Scrambled Brains

Scrambled Brains

A COOKING GUIDE FOR THE REALITY IMPAIRED

RECIPES COLLECTED AND DEVELOPED BY

Pierre LeBlanc

COMICS AND ILLUSTRATIONS BY

Robin Konstabaris

PLUS SOME STUFF THEY
WROTE TOGETHER

ARSENAL PULP PRESS
Vancouver

ARSENAL PULP PRESS
103-1014 Homer Street
Vancouver, B.C.
Canada V6B 2W9

The publisher gratefully acknowledges the assistance of the Book Publishing Industry Development Program.

Typeset by Patty Osborne, Vancouver Desktop Publishing Centre

Printed and bound in Canada

CANADIAN CATALOGUING IN PUBLICATION DATA:
Konstabaris, Robin
  Scrambled brains

  ISBN 1-55152-042-7

  1. Low budget cookery. 2. Quick and easy cookery.
I. LeBlanc, Pierre, 1964- II. Title.

TX652.K66 1997   641.5′5   C97-910741-5

Dedicated to

_____

ACKNOWLEDGEMENTS

Too numerous to mention, and besides, we're embarrassed
by how much help we needed to make this book.

Table of Contents

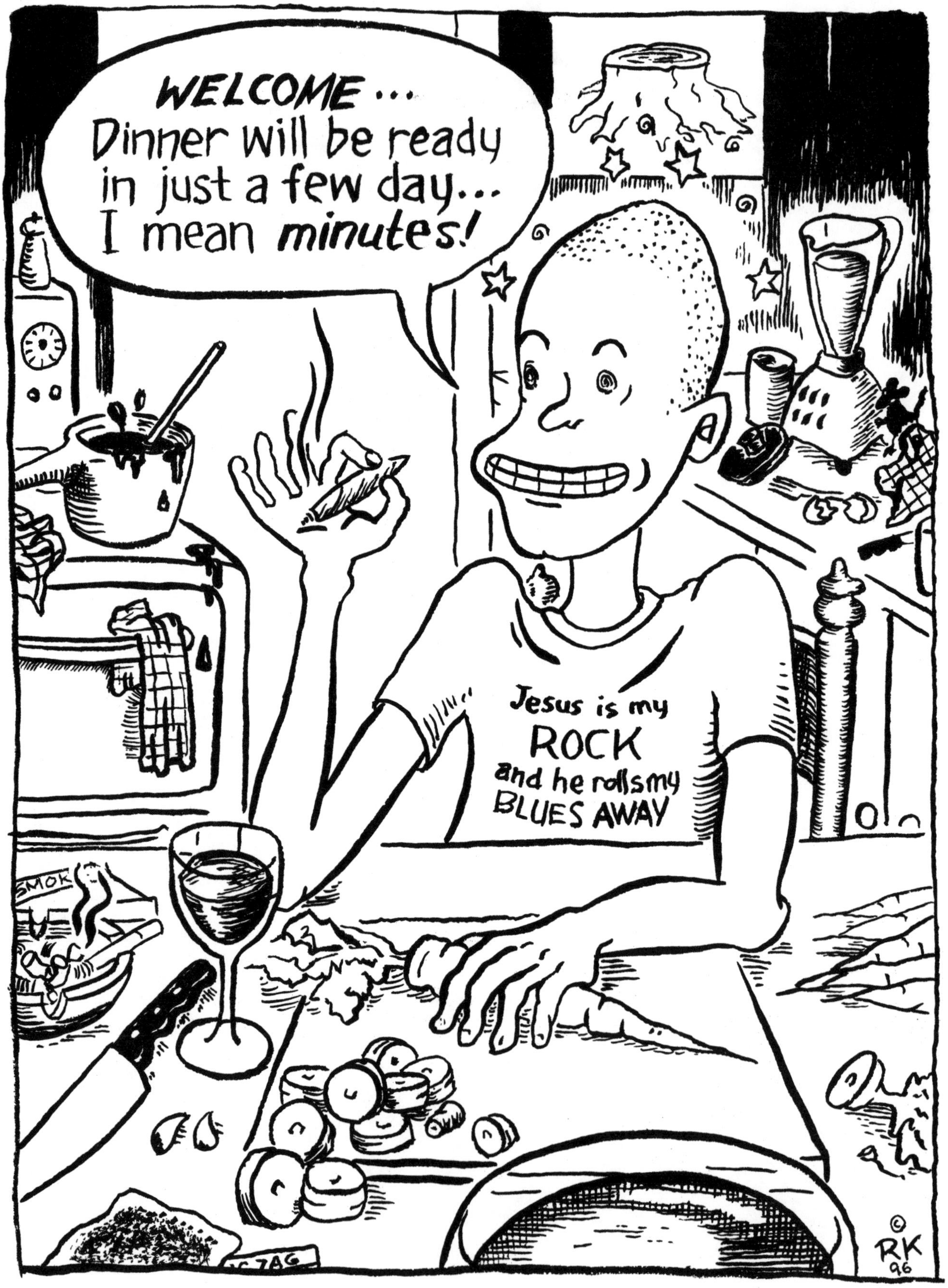
WELCOME...
Dinner will be ready in just a few day... I mean minutes!
Jesus is my ROCK and he rolls my BLUES AWAY
© RK 96

A Word From The Cook

WHAT IS SCRAMBLED BRAINS?

These days people seem to have a convoluted idea about what food is. Cheese comes from an aerosol can, sauce from an envelope, and MSG makes it all taste good. They believe that they are too busy to feed themselves unless the food is preassembled and ready in a minute. Can't they see their petri dish overfloweth?

I, Pierre LeBlanc, have decided that this must change.

I spent many isolated years at the *Scrambled Brains* Laboratory on a relentless and painstaking quest to bring you recipes that, while simple to make, surpass all known boundaries of culinary excellence. My faithful assistant Robin kept extensive visual notes and diaries of our adventures exploring the global palate. Entombed in these pages are the fruits of that labour.

Oh, reader, consider your almost incredible good luck having this venerable volume in your hands. A book that will be your guiding light on your journey to rediscovering your individual palate. Never before has such a useful and enlightening collection of recipes been assembled into one manual! (Fanfare of trumpets.)

So pick up the frying pan, check the cupboards, run to the shop for some groceries and dish soap, return to the house, pick up the frying pan again, put it down, put on that little plaid apron with the lacy edge, put on that funny looking hat, pick up the frying pan again, and let's start cooking.
It's *Scrambled Brains*.

PROLOGUE...
EAST DITCH PAWNSHOP
PAWNSHOP
GIRLS
ST. JAMES
... EARLY MORNING ON THE DOWNTOWN EASTSIDE
GOSPEL MISSIO
ROCERY
Factory Style Chicken Co.
HOTEL
Factory Style Chicken Co.
Factory Style Chick
KER CHUNK

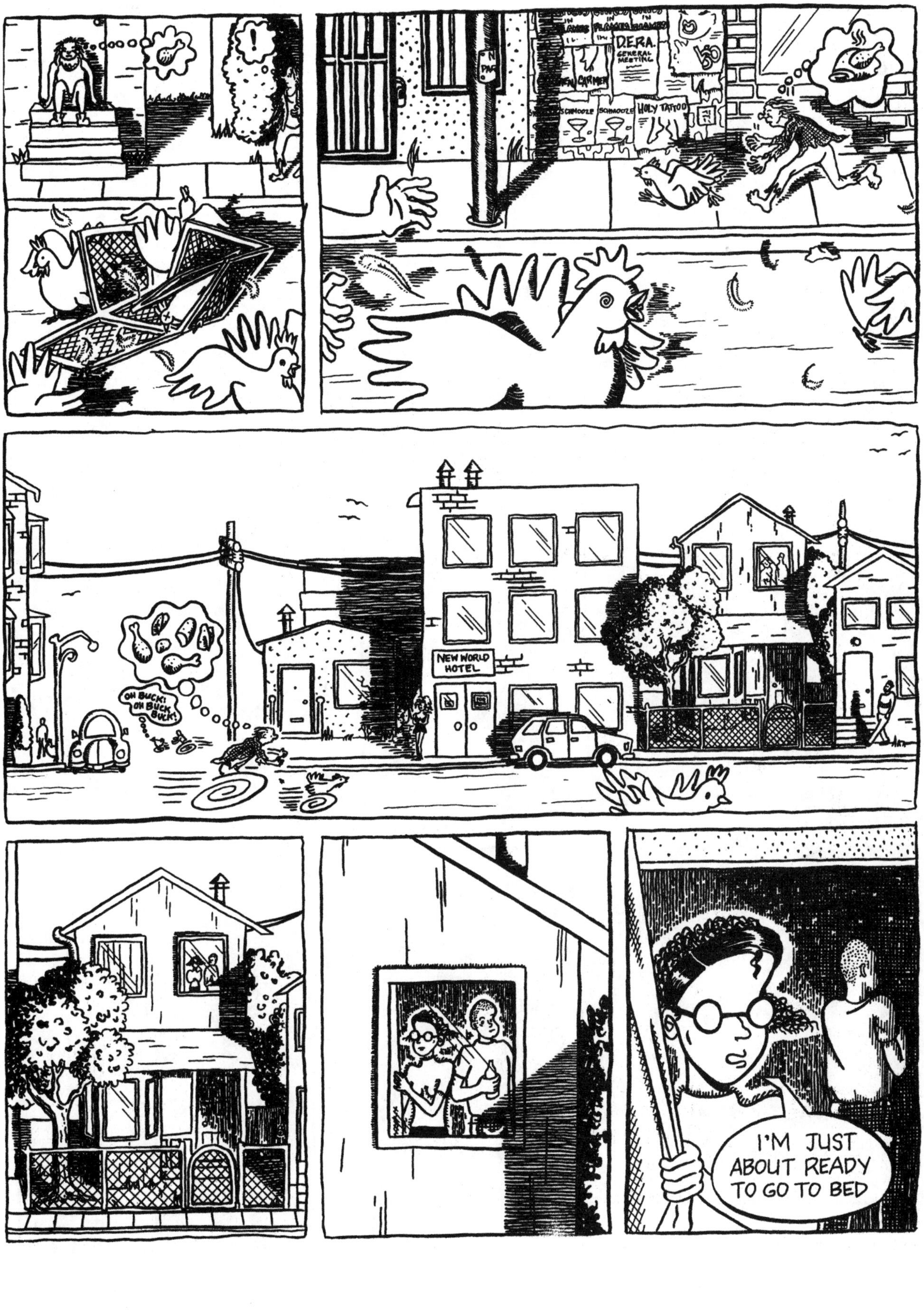
D.E.R.A.
GENERAL MEETING
CARMEN
SCHMOOZE
SCHMOOZE
HOLY TATTOO
NEW WORLD HOTEL
OH BUCK! OH BUCK BUCK!
I'M JUST ABOUT READY TO GO TO BED

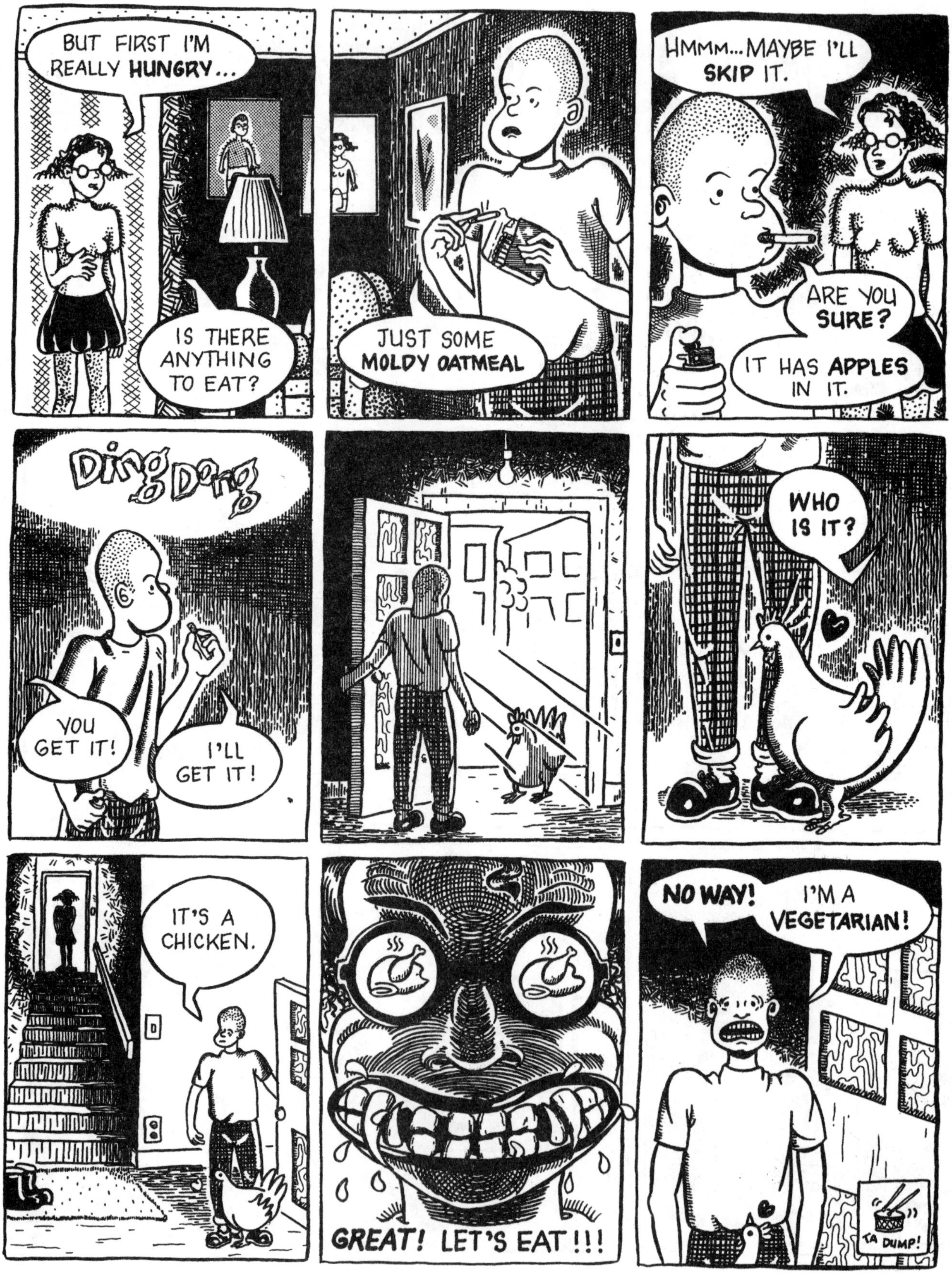
BUT FIRST I'M REALLY HUNGRY...
IS THERE ANYTHING TO EAT?
JUST SOME MOLDY OATMEAL
HMMM... MAYBE I'LL SKIP IT.
ARE YOU SURE?
IT HAS APPLES IN IT.
DING DONG
YOU GET IT!
I'LL GET IT!
WHO IS IT?
IT'S A CHICKEN.
GREAT! LET'S EAT!!!
NO WAY!
I'M A VEGETARIAN!
TA DUMP!

Poverty Kitchen

To start, challenge your impoverished taste buds with some simple and economical recipes.

The difference between eating badly and eating well on a limited budget is usually just a matter of time and care taken to prepare the meal, and a couple extra bucks spent on quality basics such as extra virgin olive oil, butter, and free range eggs. For those of you with barren cupboards it is important to stock up on staples. It is obvious that you should put your money where your mouth is, so to speak. Whatever's cheapest on the store shelf is not necessarily the best deal. Look for the most nutritious and least manipulated food products. Check expiry dates, read the labels, beware of empty calories. Or even better, avoid supermarkets and grow your own, or buy direct from farmers.

Bon appetit!

leftover Kraft Dinner® project

STEP 1: After dining on Kraft Dinner®, instead of cleaning up the kitchen, smoke a **bomber.** Then take a **plate,** clean or dirty, and on it **arrange** the leftover Kraft Dinner® into a **self expressive picture** or an **attractive pattern.**

STEP 2: Procrastinate cleaning the kitchen for 10-14 days, then **clean** the kitchen. At some point you will discover your **perfectly preserved** Kraft Dinner® artwork **dry** and **ready** for display! **Makes a great gift!**

Kraft Dinner Alternative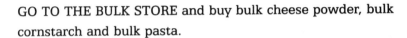

For those who crave industrial food.

1 cup pasta

3 tbsp. butter (or margarine)

1/4 cup milk

2 tbsp. cheese food powder

1 tbsp. cornstarch

salt and pepper to taste

GO TO THE BULK STORE and buy bulk cheese powder, bulk cornstarch and bulk pasta.

Boil pasta just like you boil pasta from the Kraft Dinner box. Mix the cornstarch and cheese powder together. Drain pasta and return to the pasta pot. Add butter and stir until it's melted, then add cheese powder/cornstarch mix.

Keep stirring. Add milk until desired consistency is reached. Season to taste.

Compare the price of this meal to the price of Kraft Dinner and question whether the convenience of prepackaged food is worth it to you to line the pockets of large mega-corporations.
We know, we know, you think of Kraft Dinner as "comfort food," the kind that reminds you of your childhood. But really, how comfortable are you with the profit-motivated control these corporations exercise on your government and community? Do you think they care about you or your comfort? They don't. So if you still insist on eating Kraft Dinner don't come to us looking for sympathy when your dad loses his dairy farm.

Makes as many servings as a box of Kraft Dinner would.

Kraft Dinner Alternative B

In this exciting recipe, learn the secrets of making a basic cheese sauce!

2 cups pasta

3 tbsp. flour

3 tbsp. butter

1 cup milk

1/2 cup aged cheddar cheese, grated

1 tsp. Dijon mustard (optional)

pinch of nutmeg (optional)

salt and pepper to taste

PUT PASTA WATER to boil.

Heat a saucepan to medium heat and thoroughly melt the butter, then remove it from the heat. Sift in the flour and mix in well with a wooden spoon. Return to a very low heat and let it cook 3-5 minutes, gently stirring occasionally to avoid burning. You should end up with a golden nutty tasting paste known as a "brown roux." Remove the saucepan from the heat again and slowly add the milk, stirring constantly to ensure the roux and milk are completely mixed. Return to a medium low heat and stir occasionally so the mix doesn't stick to the bottom of the pot. This sauce should thicken in about 5 minutes. Add the optional nutmeg and/or mustard. Stir in the grated cheese and remove the sauce from heat.

When the pasta is cooked, strain, let dry, and mix in sauce. Season to taste.

Makes 2 servings.

BROWN ROUX

When making a brown roux you will get a better result by letting it cook on a very low heat for a long period of time, stirring with a wooden spoon just enough to avoid burning. If you don't have a wooden spoon, go out and buy one. Over-stirring or whisking creates an overly glutenous paste that will make your sauce too heavy. Just let the flour do its thing, and it will become a golden brown roux, rewarding you with a lighter sauce with a subtle, nutty dimension.

Basic Pasta Recipe

O porco mio, Mama just can't crank out enough.

1 cup flour minus 2 tbsp.

2 tbsp. semolina

1 egg

1 tbsp. olive oil (or canola oil)

2 tsp. water

pinch of salt

IN A LARGE BOWL mix the flour and semolina and then form a well in it. Mix the liquid ingredients together, putting the salt on the egg yolk before blending. Pour the liquid into the flour well, and mixing with your hands work the flour into the liquid. When the ingredients are well mixed, knead them for 8 minutes to form a unified elastic dough. If the dough is sticky, knead in more flour. If the dough is too dry, add more water. Pat it into a ball and let it rest for 1 hour.

If you haven't run to the store for ready-made pasta by this point then it's time to roll out the dough. But first prepare your pasta water.

Be absolutely sure your rolling surface is clean and dry. Divide the dough into quarters to be rolled and cut individually. Sprinkle flour on the rolling surface and rolling pin (or bottle or whatever you're using to roll with), then roll out the dough as thinly as you can.* Using a sharp knife, cut the dough into pasta-width strips (however wide you want the noodles. You've got the power!). Place the completed pasta noodles on a dry floured plate. You have reached a crucial stage here. Do not over-manipulate the pasta or it will stick together. Perhaps sprinkle flour lightly onto the completed noodles as extra no clump insurance (there are those who claim semolina is better than flour for this). Any excess insurance flour will wash away during boiling.

When pasta water is at a complete boil, add the pasta and let it cook for about 4-5 minutes, depending on the thickness of your noodles. Stir occasionally and lightly to avoid pasta stickage.

Drain, but don't rinse, when cooked.

Makes 4 servings.

A HANDY TIP

It's best not to roll out your pasta until you're ready to cook it. You can make your sauce while the dough is resting.

*Those who own pasta rollers will tell you tales of frustration leading to the purchase of their equipment.

Pasta with Tomato, Olives, and Parmesan

A quick and easy back-of-the-fridge delight!

1 1/2 cups pasta (a chunky one; e.g., rotini, fusilli, macaroni)

1 tomato, cut into 1/4 inch cubes

12 black olives, pitted and halved

2 cloves garlic, minced

2 tbsp. butter

2 tbsp. fresh basil

Parmesan cheese to taste

salt and pepper to taste

BOIL THE PASTA and then drain it.

Heat a large fry pan to medium heat and melt the butter in it. As the butter turns brown add the garlic, tomatoes and olives. Sauté for 2 minutes. Add the basil and stir. Add the cooked pasta and stir until covered in sauce. Add salt, pepper, and Parmesan to taste.

Serves 2 people or one pig.

PREPARING PASTA: *When preparing pasta, cook it in a lot of water so it doesn't stick to itself. Add salt and oil if desired.*

Cooking time depends on the type of pasta. Short, long, thin, fat, homemade, store-bought, dried or fresh, they are all different. Sooo, you must be attentive. First let your water come to a roaring boil, stir it up really well and add the pasta. At first stir it lots to keep it from sticking together, and then occasionally. Let it cook until it's tender yet a little bit firm (al dente). (One good way of finding out if your pasta is ready is to throw it on the ceiling; if it sticks, it's cooked.) Then drain the pasta and use it immediately. Sauce sticks to the noodle better on an unrinsed pasta, and often rinsed pasta will dilute the flavours of the sauce. However, if you forget to check your pasta and it overcooks, rinsing in cold water is the only way to halt the cooking process.

WHY FRESH HERBS?

The bouquet that fresh herbs add to a recipe makes the task of creating flavourful food easy. Many people find once they start using fresh herbs and even growing them, they're hooked. Most fresh herbs freeze well, either in a mason jar or a freezer bag. You can also use an ice cube tray so that you will have an assortment of herbs to choose from. If you do use dry herbs, use them sparingly because their flavours are more concentrated. Dried marjoram and basil tend to be either bitter or bland, but dry thyme, bay leaves, and oregano retain their true flavour even when dried.

Basic Tomato Sauce (a coulis)

You say tomato, I say pomadori!

8 fresh tomatoes, diced

1 large onion, diced

4 cloves garlic, minced

3 tbsp. butter or oil

1 tbsp. fresh oregano, chopped

1 tbsp. fresh basil, chopped

splash of wine if you're drinking it at the time

salt and pepper to taste

HEAT A LARGE SKILLET over high heat until it's smoking. Add butter, onions, salt, and pepper. Sauté for 3 minutes. Add the minced garlic and stir 5 times while chanting "Mario Lanza, I love you!" Add the herbs and stir twice (no chanting necessary). Add the tomatoes and the wine if you've got it. If not, have a brief moment of self-pity, then just add the tomatoes. Simmer for 20 minutes, stirring occasionally.

Adjust seasoning to your taste. Purée. Straining optional.

Adjust the viscosity with water.

Makes about 4 cups.

SKINNING AND SEEDING

Here's a quick and easy method for skinning and seeding fresh tomatoes. Get a large pot of water to a roaring boil. Remove the stems of the tomatoes by inserting a small kitchen knife at an inward angle slightly beside the stem. Twist the knife in a circular motion to remove a cone-shaped bit containing the stem. Don't cut yourself. Turn the tomato upside down and make an x-shaped incision across the bottom, about 1 inch wide. Place the tomatoes into the boiling water for 3 minutes, or until the skin begins to peel away from the flesh. Strain the tomatoes before submerging into icy cold water. Put your hands in the cold water and remove the skin.

To remove the seeds, slice the tomatoes in half and over a bowl pick out the seeds with a spoon, then strain the seeds to recover the lost juices. And voilà! Your very own skinned and seeded tomatoes, ready for soups, sauces, and concassés.

Tomato and Lentil Sauce for Pasta

Nice served with grilled patra (opposite).

1 cup water

1 cup small red lentils, dry

6 tomatoes, diced (or 1 tin stewed tomatoes)

1 onion, diced

3 cloves garlic, minced

2 raw beet roots cut into small cubes

juice of 1 lemon

2 tbsp. canola oil

1 tbsp. dried cumin

1 tsp. fennel seed

1/2 tsp. cayenne pepper

1 tsp. fresh ginger, minced (or 1 tsp. ginger powder)

salt and pepper to taste

MIX THE WATER and lemon juice together and place the cubed beets in it. Set it aside to soak.

Heat the oil in a saucepan over high heat. Add the onions and a pinch of salt and sauté 3 minutes, then add the garlic, fennel seed, cumin, cayenne pepper, and ginger and cook another 3 minutes, stirring constantly. Add the tomatoes and crush them, crush them, crush them with the wooden spoon. Add the beets and lemon water and bring it all to a boil. Reduce the heat to medium low and simmer for 15 minutes. Add the lentils and cook for 25 minutes on the medium low heat. Season to taste.

Serve over a hardy noodle such as buckwheat, curried, or whole wheat. Accompany with grilled patra, and yoghurt on the side.

Makes 4-6 servings.

Grilled Patra

Not to be advocates of packaged food, but in Little India we discovered patra, one of the yummiest things ever served from a can.

The name "patra" comes from the Indian word "patte," meaning "leaf." The leaves of the taro root are blanched and then laid out in sheets. Spread on top is a mixture composed of chick pea flour and spices, then the whole thing is rolled like a pinwheel and steamed.

1 can patra

little bit of sesame oil

little bit of sesame seeds

CUT THE PATRA into thin slices, then rub on a wee bit of sesame oil and a sprinkle of sesame seeds. Keep in mind the flavour of the sesame oil is very strong, so a little bit is fine.

Place under the grill 'til they are nice and golden brown.

Makes 1 can.

THE PATRA SECRET

There is one can-sized pinwheel of patra fitted into each tin. How do they get the patra in like that? It's an industrial mystery.

We here at Scrambled Brains can't tell you how it got into the can, but here's a handy tip on how to get it out of the can: open the tin on both ends, then carefully push on one end with either the can lid or your fingers to remove the pinwheel intact.

These vegan rolls are very popular in India, where they are usually prepared by sautéing them with mustard seeds.

Risotto

The great risotto debate: is the consistency supposed to be dry and fluffy, or wet and mucky? The French chef says it is dry and fluffy. The Italian chef says it is wet and mucky. We say, "Shut up and eat, you overpaid, egocentric bastards! And we'll stir it if we want to!"

3 cups Vegetable Broth, pg. 39

1 cup rizzo (Arborio rice, an Italian short-grain rice)

1 tomato, cut in concassé

1 onion, finely diced

1 carrot, finely diced

1 red bell pepper, finely diced

1 stick of celery, finely diced

1 clove garlic, minced

1 tbsp. fresh chopped oregano

2 tbsp. fresh chopped basil

3 tbsp. olive oil

salt and pepper to taste

IN A SMALL BOWL mix the tomatoes, oregano, and basil and set it aside.

Heat a large, deep skillet over high heat until it smokes. Add the oil, onions, and salt and sauté for 2 minutes. Add the carrots, celery, bell pepper, and garlic and sauté for a further 3 minutes, stirring constantly. Add the rice and stir in thoroughly. The oil will coat the rice, causing it to become somewhat translucent. This prevents the rice from soaking up too much moisture, and the risotto from turning out mushy.

Still over the high heat, let the rice sit without stirring for 30 seconds, then add 1/2 cup of the vegetable broth and reduce the heat to medium low. Stir and continue to stir every now and then. After about 3-5 minutes the broth should evaporate and then it's time to add another 1/2 cup of vegetable broth to be stirred and evaporated. Keep repeating this until only 1/2 cup of the broth remains.

Stir in the tomato and the herbs. Add the remaining broth and let cook for 5 more minutes.

Season to taste.

Right before eating throw in a splash of cream and some shaved Parmesan. Serve with sautéed mushrooms.

Makes 2-4 servings.

POVERTY HUMOUR

"Tell me a funny story about poverty, Pierre."

"I can't Robin. There is nothing funny about poverty."

Garbanzo con Espinacas

Chickpeas with spinach.

A HANDY TIP

Don't forget to soak the garbanzo beans overnight.

2 cups soaked garbanzo beans

8 cups water

4 cups fresh spinach, shredded

1 white onion, finely diced

2 tbsp. olive oil (or canola oil)

2 tbsp. celery leaf and /or leaf parsley

pinch of nutmeg

pinch of cayenne pepper

salt and pepper to taste

BOIL THE GARBANZO BEANS in the water for 1 1/2 hours, and don't let the pot boil dry. Meanwhile you should find the time to prepare other ingredients and maybe catch up on some household chores. Please don't leave the house while the stove is on.

When the beans are ready, drain them and discard the water. Heat a skillet over high heat until it's smoking. Add the oil, onions, and salt and cook and stir for 3 minutes (that's a sauté, in case you still don't know). Add the garbanzos, cayenne pepper, and nutmeg, and again sauté for 3 minutes. Add the spinach and herbs and keep sautéing until all the juice has been released from the spinach, or 2 minutes, whichever comes first.

Makes 4 servings.

Pinto Beans with Pumpkin

Frijoles con Calabaza.

6 cups water

3 cups pinto beans, soaked overnight

2 cups fresh Calabaza pumpkin flesh, diced into fine cubes

1 large onion, diced

2 cloves garlic, minced

2 tbsp. tomato paste

2 tbsp. olive oil (or canola oil)

2 tsp. chili powder

1/2 tsp. cinnamon

salt and pepper to taste

IN A LARGE HEAVY POT sauté the onions in the olive oil for 3 minutes. Add the pinto beans, pumpkin, garlic, chili powder, and cinnamon. Add the 6 cups of water and bring to a boil. Reduce the heat to low, and cook covered for an hour, stirring every 15-20 minutes. Remove the lid from the pot and turn up the heat to medium, to allow the liquid to reduce by half. Stir while reducing until pumpkin is thoroughly broken down and stirred to a sauce-like texture.

Add the tomato paste and salt and cook over low heat for another 20 minutes, stirring so it doesn't stick. Season to taste. After all this, if the beans aren't cooked, rip this page from the book and discard.

Makes a pot of beans.

CALABAZA

Also known as West Indian pumpkin, green pumpkin, ahuyama, zapallo, and abobora. Calabaza is a winter squash that is most easily acquired from shops which specialize in Caribbean or Latin American foodstuffs. If for some reason (like, say, laziness) you are unable to obtain this ingredient, a butternut or marrow squash makes an acceptable substitute.

the CHICKEN Came to Stay

PIERRE! THAT CHICKEN IS **STILL** HERE!

I KEEP FINDING EGGS

... BUT I CAN'T FIND THE CHICKEN.

Yuk! THERE'S CHICKEN #?@! ON THE FLOOR!

NOW I CAN FILL THE **BATHTUB** WITH **MAYONNAISE** FOR MY DATE TONIGHT!

WAIT. THERE'S MORE...

Mayonnaise

We may be white trash, but we know how to make our own mayonnaise.

3 egg yolks

1 1/4 cups canola oil

1/2 cup olive oil (or 1/2 cup more canola oil)

3 tbsp. lemon juice

1 tbsp. vinegar

salt and pepper to taste

PUT EGG YOLKS, lemon juice, and vinegar into a large bowl, and mix together with a whisk. You must have a whisk for this recipe. You need to become a human whisking machine. When the stuff is whisked, start adding the oil. At first dribble it in one tablespoon at a time, whisking thoroughly between each oil increment. The consistency should be thickening and the sauce turning white. As the mayonnaise thickens it can absorb more oil, so you can increase the increments of oil as you get further along. Keep whisking! When all the oil is whisked in you're more or less done, unless you'd like to add more lemon juice or some salt and pepper. If you'd like that then go ahead and add them.

Your mayonnaise is now complete.

In an airtight container, it will keep in the fridge for about a week.

Makes 2 cups.

SALTING: *Call it an old wives' tale, but we always salt our yolks. Somehow recipes seem to require less salt when it is applied this way.*

Aioli

This garlic mayonnaise recipe is a variation of the original French aioli, which is traditionally made with minced raw garlic mixed in with the yolks before the making of the mayonnaise. En Provence, you start with two cloves of garlic per person.

1 cup mayonnaise, pg. 18

1 whole bulb of garlic

1 tbsp. olive oil (or canola oil)

1/4 cup lemon juice

salt and pepper to taste

PLACE THE WHOLE BULB of garlic on a piece of tin foil and dribble the olive oil over it. Wrap the foil completely around the garlic bulb and roast in the oven at 350° for 30-40 minutes. The cooked garlic will become sort of pasty and the skin will remove easily. Remove the skin and let the garlic cool.

In a bowl, whisk together the garlic, mayonnaise, and lemon juice. Season to taste.

Use on anything you would normally use mayo on. A tip for sadists: try rubbing it all over your vampire lover.

Makes 1 1/2 cups.

Caesar Salad Dressing

3/4 cup mayonnaise, pg. 18

1/4 cup lemon juice

1/4 cup olive oil

3-4 cloves of garlic, minced

2-3 anchovy fillets, patted dry and chopped finely

1 tbsp. capers, crushed

4 drops tabasco sauce

1 tbsp. white wine vinegar

fresh ground pepper

PLACE IN A BOWL the mayonnaise, lemon juice, and vinegar. Whisk. Add the garlic, anchovies, and capers. Whisk. Put the olive oil and tabasco sauce in. Whisk. Finish off with freshly ground pepper.

You are welcome to play with the proportions of flavourful ingredients to modify to taste.

Makes 1 1/2 cups.

Croutons

3 cups of dry bread scraps cut into nice big cubes

4 cloves of garlic, finely minced

1/4 cup butter

salt and pepper to taste

MELT THE BUTTER in a large skillet over low heat. Stir in the garlic and let it sit for 3 minutes, leaving the heat on. This lets the garlic flavour expand and infuse into the butter. Bring the heat up to medium high, being careful not to burn the garlic. Add the bread cubes and toss them vigorously with 2 wooden spoons, ensuring the cubes are evenly coated with butter.

Then follow 1 of 2 methods:

1. **Classic French Croutons**: Reduce the heat to medium low, then keep stirring and tossing constantly until the croutons become crispy and golden brown. (Pierre's preferred method.)

2. **Slutty American Cretins**: Place the buttered bread cubes on a cookie sheet and bake in a 375° oven for 5-8 minutes.

Caesar Salad in 3 easy steps

Makes one big Caesar Salad.

1 head of Romaine leaf lettuce

1/2 cup Caesar dressing, pg. 20

Croutons, pg. 20

1/4 cup Parmesan cheese

1 lemon

2 tbsp. vinegar

salt and pepper to taste

Step 1: Fill a clean sink with icy cold water and add the vinegar (this kills whatever keeps you up at night). Cut a 1/2 inch off the bottom of the lettuce and break it apart. Soak it in the water for at least 5 minutes. Rip the leaves into bite-sized pieces and place them in a colander. The best leaves are the smallest ones, so if you're not going to use the whole head of lettuce, choose those for the salad. Place the colander of lettuce in a large salad bowl, cover with a clean cloth and refrigerate for 20 minutes to crisp the lettuce.

Step 2: Discard the chilled water in the bottom of the salad bowl and dump the lettuce into the bowl. Add the juice of one lemon. Toss a few times and add the croutons. Toss a few times and add the Parmesan. Toss a few times and add the Caesar salad dressing. Toss a few times. Sprinkle with fresh ground pepper.

Step 3: Eat it.

A HANDY PAGAN TIP

If you are using non-organic lettuce, discard the outer leaves or save for midnight rituals.

Tortilla de Patatas

"Why, I haven't had such a tasty tortilla since I was in Sevilla!"
–an anonymous connoisseur

6 eggs

3 potatoes, fanned (see illustration below)

1 large white onion, diced

1 stick of celery, finely chopped

1/4 cup olive oil

1 tsp. baking powder

1/4 tsp. mustard powder

1/4 tsp. paprika

1/4 tsp. cayenne pepper

1/8 tsp. thyme

salt and pepper to taste

QUARTER THE POTATOES lengthwise and cut into 1/8-inch fans, then steam them for 3 minutes.

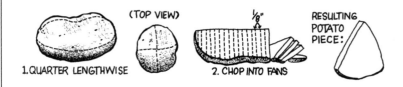

Don't rinse them, just let them sit.

Make a large cast-iron skillet smoking hot, then add 3/4 of the 1/4 cup of olive oil. Sauté the onion, celery and a pinch of salt for 3 minutes. Stir in the potatoes, 2 pinches of salt, mustard, thyme, paprika, and half of the cayenne pepper and sauté over a medium high heat for 15 minutes. It is preferable to shake the pan rather than stirring the contents so as not to crumble the potatoes. Gently turn the potatoes over to get them evenly cooked. If they start to stick you can add a wee bit more oil.

While this is happening, crack the 6 eggs into a bowl and add a few pinches of salt, the rest of the cayenne pepper, and the baking powder, then beat it until it's fluffy.

(If you are not using a cast-iron pan, or if your potatoes are very starchy, you might find you have to remove them, then clean and re-season the pan before going on to the next step. Don't laze out on this, or all your tortilla dreams will come to naught.)

Ensure the potato fans are evenly distributed in the skillet and pour the egg mixture over top. Reduce the heat to low and cook without stirring for 15 minutes.

You may want to run a knife around the edge of the pan to make sure the sides of the tortilla don't stick, then flip the tortilla like this: take a plate large enough to cover the pan and place it upside down on the pan. Holding it firmly in place with one hand, lift the pan with your other hand (don't forget your oven mitt) and very carefully turn everything over so the tortilla ends up cooked side up on the plate. Be sure to use a gentle yet forceful approach.

Using the remaining olive oil, season the pan (see below), then slide the tortilla off the plate into the pan, cooked side up. Cook over low heat for another 15 minutes. Season to taste.

Traditionally served cold, but some like it warm.

VARIATIONS: Once you've mastered the classic tortilla, try adding tuna, roasted bell peppers, or even chorizo.

Makes 8-10 slices.

SEASONING CAST-IRON FRYING PANS: *Place the clean pan over high heat until it starts to smoke. Wipe the inside of the pan with an oiled rag (use edible oil products only, please).*

Robin's Potato Pancake

"For some reason I've never been able to successfully make this recipe on an electric stove."
—a highly-paid researcher from the *Scrambled Brains* laboratory

1 medium sized potato, grated

1/2 medium sized onion, grated

2-3 tbsp. flour

1-2 tbsp. butter or oil

salt and pepper to taste

MIX EVERYTHING except the butter in a large bowl. Heat a medium-sized cast-iron frying pan over high heat, melt the butter in it and reduce the heat to medium low. We usually use a lot of butter, but for the health conscious a little will do, or use oil. Dump the potato mix into the pan and pack it down uniformly into one large patty. Cook uncovered for 10-15 minutes, or until the bottom side is golden brown, then flip it with a spatula. If the pancake is cooked enough it should hold together without a problem, so if it sticks to the pan or starts to fall apart, try cooking it a bit more. Cook the other side until brown. Season to taste.

Top with salsa or sour cream or anything in the fridge. Yum, yum. Hot sauce is nice.

Makes 1 serving.

Tempeh with Kecap Manis

We've never had a meat lover turn their nose up at this vegan dish.

1 block of tempeh, cut into 1/8" cubes

1/4 cup canola oil

1/2 cup kecap manis (sweet soy sauce)

3 cloves garlic, minced

1/2 fresh chili, finely chopped

1/2 tbsp. fresh ginger (or laos), minced

2 tbsp. fresh cilantro, chopped

splash of lemon juice

salt to taste

IN A SMALL SAUCEPAN mix the kecap manis, garlic, ginger, chili, and lemon juice. Place over low heat and leave to simmer so the flavours can infuse.

Pour the oil into a cast-iron skillet over high heat. When the oil is properly heated, add the tempeh and a generous pinch of salt. Maintaining a medium heat and stirring frequently, fry for about 5 minutes, or until the tempeh is a nice golden brown. Remove from heat and use a perforated spoon or spatula to remove the tempeh from the pan. Place them on a paper towel (or a large paper bag) to soak up the excess fat.

Mix the sauce and the tempeh together. Add the cilantro before serving.

Accompany with steamed vegetables and rice.

Makes 4 servings.

WHAT IS TEMPEH?

Tempeh is a meat substitute made of cooked soya beans and some kind of fermenting agent. The beans and the fermenting agent are placed to incubate until they solidify into blocks. To Robin it looks like tofu. Pierre thinks it looks more like brie.

Tempeh is commonly used in Indonesian cooking, and is usually sold frozen at health food stores and some Asian markets. But buy only fresh or frozen tempeh, which will be white. As it ages, it discolours to a bluish-grey.

CRUMBLE CRUST

1/2 cup brown sugar

1/2 cup butter

1 cup rolled oats

pinch of salt

IN A SKILLET, melt butter and sugar over medium high heat until the sugar begins to melt. Add oats and salt, stir vigorously for 3 minutes, and use immediately.

Did You Think I'd Crumble?

This recipe is dedicated to those suffering from unrequited love.

6-8 apples, peeled, cored, and halved

3 cups water

3 cups apple juice

1 lemon, sliced

3 cloves (stick them into the lemon and think evil thoughts while singing the "Lovely Lemon Tree" song [optional])

2 star anise (optional)

1 tsp. pure vanilla extract or 1 vanilla bean

1 tsp. fresh ginger (or 1 tsp. ginger powder)

1/4 cup sugar

pinch of salt

IN A LARGE POT over high heat pour the water and apple juice, then add the lemon slices, star anise, vanilla, ginger, sugar, and salt, and bring to a boil. Place the apples in the boiling liquid, then reduce the heat to low and let poach for 10-15 minutes or until tender but firm. Remove apples (and strain poaching liquid for a scrumptious vodka cocktail). Place apples on a greased 9" x 9" (approx.) baking dish and cover with crumble crust mixture (see sidebar). Bake at 350° for 25 minutes.

Makes 4-6 servings.

Blackberry Pie

Turn off the TV, leave the house, and go pick blackberries. If it's wintertime you're off the hook, but you get no pie.

2 lbs. blackberries

1 cup sugar

pinch of salt

juice of one lime or lemon (optional)

1 Short Pie Crust, pg. 28

WASH THE BERRIES and set half aside. Place the other half in a saucepan with the sugar and the optional juice of one lime or lemon. Bring to a full boil, stirring occasionally. Let the mixture reduce by half to become a thick syrup. Place the reserved uncooked berries into a short crust pie shell (see following page). The berries should not exceed half the pie shell. Pour the syrup over the top, and cover with a lattice made with pie dough (see pg. 29). Bake at 350° for 35 minutes. It is a good idea to place a cookie sheet on the rack below the pie in the oven as a precaution against escaped berry juice.

Makes 1 pie.

ADVICE FOR ARACHNIPHOBES:

Blackberry-picking arachniphobes beware: There's spiders in them there bushes! But don't let them deter you. They can be controlled by materials at hand.

Our arachniphobic friend Kate, on a berry-picking venture in Mission, B.C., dealt with the copious spiders with a Spider Stick. The Spider Stick, indigenous to the ground of most rural and wild areas, is available in a variety of shapes and sizes. Its many uses include breaking and removing spider webs, and also brushing large spiders away.

For extra confidence and vigour while using the Spider Stick, sing this popular song: (to the tune of "Spider Man")

Spider chick, spider chick,
Deals with it with a
 Spider Stick

Feel free to invent new words to suit your individual circumstances.

AN EXAMPLE OF A TYPICAL PACIFIC NORTHWESTERN SPIDER STICK

Short Pie Crust

. . . with a tall pie crust attitude!

2 1/4 cups flour

1/2 cup white sugar

1 cup butter, at room temperature

1 egg, beaten

4-6 tbsp. ice water

pinch of salt

FLAKING OUT

When preparing pastry, the amount of liquid needed to form the dough may vary depending on the type of flour you are using, and its freshness. As a general guideline, if your dough is too crumbly, add more water in 1-tablespoon increments until proper consistency is achieved.

MIX FLOUR, SUGAR, and salt in a bowl. Cut butter up into small cubes and add the cubes to the dry ingredients. Mix by cutting with a pastry cutter or two knives. Don't use your hands for this part because your body heat will melt the butter, resulting in a tough crust. When the butter is broken down into small pea size chunks, add the egg, salt, and water. Quickly mix together with your hands and form into a ball. Refrigerate for 40 minutes before using.

Prepare a dry, clean surface to work on. Dust the surface and the rolling pin with flour. Use 2/3 of the dough for the bottom crust, reserving 1/3 for the top. Now, roll to the east and roll to the west, and think about the one that you love best. If there is no one, cry. Now, roll to the south and roll to the north, and think of the one you want to divorce. Ah ha ha ha. Dust the dough, flip, and dust again. Now that we've developed a compass to roll the dough, roll NE to SE, then NW to SW, to make the pastry form a circle. Always start rolling from the middle and work outwards. If your dough begins to crack at the edges, pinch it together with your fingers.

Roll it out large enough to fit your pie plate. Grease the pie plate. Place the rolling pin on the centre of the dough circle and flip one side over it so you can lift the crust with the rolling pin. This should help you get the crust from the work surface to the pie plate. Press the dough to the plate, and trim the excess dough from the edges, leaving a bit overhanging to make the pinched crust edge if desired.

LATTICED CRUST: *For a berry pie like the one on page 27, it is preferable to have a "semi-open" or latticed top crust. A whole top crust makes the pie too runny, and no crust makes it dry.*

Take the scraps and reserved dough and roll it into a rectangle. Cut it into 8-10 uniform strips, then follow the simple self explanatory illustration below. After you have completed the easy lattice, either pinch the ends of the strips to the edge of the bottom crust, or brush with a beaten egg.

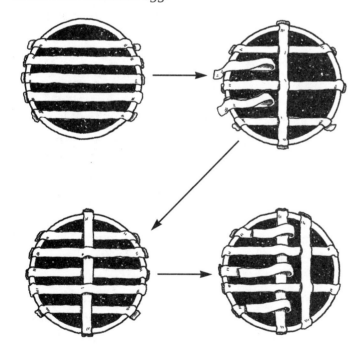

Farts, anyone?

A POINT OF HISTORICAL INTEREST

In the old days, the fat of freshly slaughtered chicken was sometimes used instead of shortening in the making of this recipe.

Nun's Farts

(Pets de Soeurs)

Eglantine's recipe — a traditional Acadian treat!

CARAMEL:

1 cup brown sugar

1/2 cup warm or hot water

DOUGH:

3 cups white flour

3/4 cup vegetable shortening (like Crisco)

1 egg, beaten, plus enough milk to make one cup

4 tsp. baking powder

1 tsp. salt

FILLING:

1 cup brown sugar

1/4 cup butter at room temperature

Preheat your oven to 350°.

Step 1:

THE CARAMEL: In a 9" x 13" greased baking pan, mix together the brown sugar and hot water with a fork until the sugar crystals have broken down. Leave the mixture to sit on the stove. The heat from the oven will keep it warm and help the sugar to break down.

Step 2:

THE DOUGH: In a mixing bowl, combine the dry dough ingredients, then cut in the shortening with a pastry cutter or two knives (please don't use your hands for this part), until the shortening chunks are the size of small peas. Form a well in the mix and add the egg/milk mixture. Mix together first with a fork and then with your hands to form a ball. Divide the dough into halves, then roll each piece out into a rectangle about a 1/4-inch thick, and about 8" x 10" large.

Step 3:

THE FILLING: Spread the room temperature butter evenly over both pieces of dough, then spread the brown sugar onto that. Roll each piece width-wise (that's the shorter side) into a log. If the dough crumbles while rolling, pinch it together to show it who's God.

Slice each log into 8 pieces, about 1-inch thick.

Go get your pan with the caramel mixture, and place the slices in it. You want the syrup to be on both sides of the slices (a.k.a. "farts"), so either baste the tops with the caramel mix, or turn the slices over in it. Leave about a 1/4-inch empty space between the farts and the edges of the pan. If there is caramel left over, make sure it is evenly distributed around the farts.

Chuck it in the oven and cook for 30 minutes.

When they're cooked, they become one big fart, so with a knife slice between the farts to reinstate their individual status. Also run the knife between the farts and the edge of the pan.

Flip them over onto a large platter or heat resistant surface. The caramel is now on top. Scrape any excess caramel from the pan and dab it onto the farts.

Do not bow to temptation. Let them cool before you eat them.

Makes 16 farts.

POUTINE?
QU'EST-CE QUE C'EST?

Although in Quebec poutine *is a well-known fast food of French fries topped with cheese curds and gravy, there are those who have a different opinion. Acadian* poutine *consists of a mixture of raw and cooked potatoes stuffed with salted pork and boiled for several hours, while in Nice, France,* poutine *is a fish dish made with sardines and anchovies.*

Dirty Old Holes?

WILL THE REAL *PETS DE SOEURS* PLEASE STAND UP?

Once Pierre and Robin hosted a pover-tea party where they served traditional Acadian Nun's Farts and Dirty Old Holes.

"Farts, anyone?" asked Pierre, with a tray of Nun's Farts in his hand.

"Dirty Old Holes?" offered Robin.

One of the guests passionately insisted Robin's tray of baked apple dumplings were *Pets de Soeurs**, the authentic Quebecois dish. Then another more worldly guest reminisced of eating *Pets de Nonnes***, a *choux* pastry fritter typical of the Provence region in France. Yet another guest contended, "I'm a Maritimer and those are not Nun's Farts—they're Pope's Arses!" Another one said, "I'm also Acadian, and those are *Bourriques de Vierges****!" "No," screamed another, "they're *Bourriques de Vieilles*****!"

"What kind of anally-repressed culture could produce such crude names for a pastry? We all know they're called Yankee Buns!" This guest belched. "Oh, pardon my French!"

"Is that supposed to be some kind of a joke?" asked the worldly guest angrily.

The Nun's Farts had fuelled a dispute, not only with their questionable cultural origin and name, but with their high sugar content. What had started as a pleasant afternoon tea turned into a heated political ferment. "*Vive la France Libre!*" screeched the *Pets de Nonnes* connoisseur.

"Who the f#$k cares?" rejoined the belching guest, and threw a sizzling hot Dirty Old Hole at the Eurocentric fritter-eater.

"*Enculé******!" he cried as the molten chocolate hit his cheek. He rose and punched the Yankee in the nose.

Pierre burst into tears.

"Now look what you've done!" said Robin, who had been quiet until now. "Everybody out!"

They looked at her with confusion.

"I've heard there's some authentic *poutine* at the Deli down the road," she explained in desperation.

Pierre and Robin stayed home to clean the pover-tea mess, so they didn't witness what happened at the corner deli, but the next day it had burned down.

*Nun's farts
**Nun's farts
***Virgin's ass, or Virgin's belly button
****Old lady's ass
*****Bugger

SPACE CADETS in Dining Out

BY ROBIN KONSTABARIS — EATING PRESERVATIVES KEEPS YOU LOOKING YOUNGER LONGER

 HORK

 I'M STILL HUNGRY

 WELL, YOU ATE THE LAST POTATO

 ISN'T THERE ANYTHING ELSE?

 JUST SOME MAYONNAISE AND A SLIMY BLACK BANANA PEEL

 EELG

 BUT, AS I WAS ABOUT TO SAY BEFORE YOU SO RUDELY STOLE THE LAST POTATO, I GOT PAID TODAY, SO WE CAN GO OUT TO EAT

 WHOOHEE LET'S GO!

 I'M READY

 WILL YOU DRIVE?

 NO. I DON'T KNOW HOW TO DRIVE

 THIS LOOKS GOOD — DINER

 WHAT'S THE SPECIAL TODAY?

 ALL YOU CAN EAT $6.95 100% DAILY INTAKE OF UNKNOWN FIBERS — WATER...$7 — RAYON ACRYLIC POLYESTER SPANDEX NYLON POLYMAR LATEX

 I'LL HAVE THE LATEX

 BON D'JEUX! ALL THEY SERVE HERE ARE ARTIFICIAL FIBERS

 ? AHH! IS THAT A CHICKEN?

 BUKOV

 AHH! GET OUT! OUT! TAKE YOUR FILTHY DISEASE RIDDEN CHICKEN WITH YOU!

 HOW DID THAT CHICKEN GET HERE? THAT F@#KEN CHICKEN

 BUT ALL THEY HAD WAS SYNTHETIC FIBERS

 I HATE THAT CHICKEN!

 ? I FORGOT MY WALLET ANYWAY. MAYBE I CAN COOK SOMETHING AT HOME

 LIKE WHAT? FRIED BLACK BANANA PEEL AND CHICKEN?

 WAIT! WE FORGOT THE CHICKEN! GO BACK!

 I CAN'T! THE REVERSE IS JAMMED!

 The chicken is the spawn of Satan — DINER — BERK

Tarte Tatin aux Poires

For you monolinguists this is an upside-down pear pie.

1 Short Pie Crust, pg. 28

6-8 pears, peeled, cored, and halved

1/4 cup butter

1/4 cup brown sugar

pinch of salt

DIRTY OLD HOLES

Use your excess pie dough to make Dirty Old Holes.

Take two apples, cored and peeled. Fill the holes with chocolate hazelnut spread, wrap it with leftover pastry dough and puncture the top. Let bake for 35 minutes at 350°. When they come out you'll say, "Now I understand why they're called Dirty Old Holes."

IN A CAST-IRON pan (or oven-resistant pan), melt the butter, sugar, and salt over medium low heat, stirring constantly until the sugar has dissolved and become a caramel. Remove from heat.

Place the pears round side down (or flat side up) into the pan in a circular pattern. Don't touch the caramel. It burns, don't you know?

Roll out the short crust and place it over the pears, then cut away the excess dough. Puncture the crust with a fork to allow excess liquid to evaporate. You may want to write your secrets, spells, or obnoxious words and images on it as this will be the bottom of the pie *so no one will ever know.* Bake at 350° for 30-35 minutes.

Let it cool for 30 minutes, then using oven mitts flip it onto the plate (refer to the Tortilla de Patatas, pg. 22, for preferred flipping method). We would suggest you do this over the sink, as juice will come out and make a mess.

Makes 6-8 portions.

Soup Line Favourites

A soup is an inanimate object, yet it somehow comes to reflect the hands that manipulate it. Whether robust, savoury, bitter, sweet, intense or bland, soups have a personality too. So don't hurt them, nurture them!

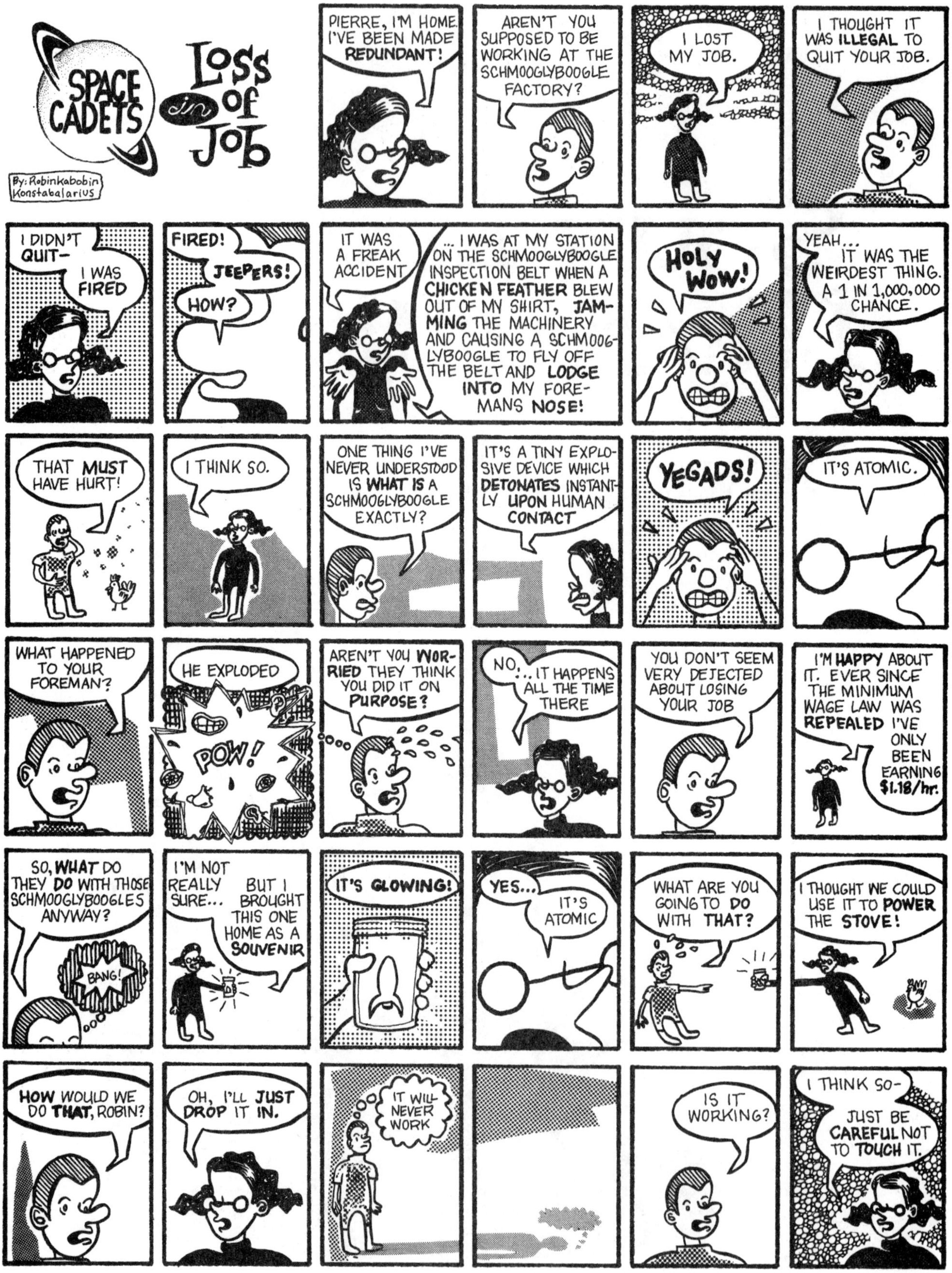
SPACE CADETS
LOSS in OF JOB
By: Robinkabobin Konstabalarius
PIERRE, I'M HOME. I'VE BEEN MADE REDUNDANT!
AREN'T YOU SUPPOSED TO BE WORKING AT THE SCHMOOGLYBOOGLE FACTORY?
I LOST MY JOB.
I THOUGHT IT WAS ILLEGAL TO QUIT YOUR JOB.
I DIDN'T QUIT-
I WAS FIRED
FIRED!
JEEPERS!
HOW?
IT WAS A FREAK ACCIDENT
... I WAS AT MY STATION ON THE SCHMOOGLYBOOGLE INSPECTION BELT WHEN A CHICKEN FEATHER BLEW OUT OF MY SHIRT, JAMMING THE MACHINERY AND CAUSING A SCHMOOGLYBOOGLE TO FLY OFF THE BELT AND LODGE INTO MY FOREMANS NOSE!
HOLY WOW!
YEAH...
IT WAS THE WEIRDEST THING. A 1 IN 1,000,000 CHANCE.
THAT MUST HAVE HURT!
I THINK SO.
ONE THING I'VE NEVER UNDERSTOOD IS WHAT IS A SCHMOOGLYBOOGLE EXACTLY?
IT'S A TINY EXPLOSIVE DEVICE WHICH DETONATES INSTANTLY UPON HUMAN CONTACT
YEGADS!
IT'S ATOMIC.
WHAT HAPPENED TO YOUR FOREMAN?
HE EXPLODED
POW!
AREN'T YOU WORRIED THEY THINK YOU DID IT ON PURPOSE?
NO,
... IT HAPPENS ALL THE TIME THERE
YOU DON'T SEEM VERY DEJECTED ABOUT LOSING YOUR JOB
I'M HAPPY ABOUT IT. EVER SINCE THE MINIMUM WAGE LAW WAS REPEALED I'VE ONLY BEEN EARNING $1.18/hr.
SO, WHAT DO THEY DO WITH THOSE SCHMOOGLYBOOGLES ANYWAY?
BANG!
I'M NOT REALLY SURE...
BUT I BROUGHT THIS ONE HOME AS A SOUVENIR
IT'S GLOWING!
YES...
IT'S ATOMIC
WHAT ARE YOU GOING TO DO WITH THAT?
I THOUGHT WE COULD USE IT TO POWER THE STOVE!
HOW WOULD WE DO THAT, ROBIN?
OH, I'LL JUST DROP IT IN.
IT WILL NEVER WORK
IS IT WORKING?
I THINK SO-
JUST BE CAREFUL NOT TO TOUCH IT.

 NOW THAT YOU'VE **LOST YOUR JOB,** WHAT ARE YOU GOING TO DO FOR **MONEY?**

 WELL, I WROTE ALL THESE STORIES WHICH I **ADAPTED** FROM MY **DIARIES,** SO I THOUGHT I WOULD HAVE THEM PUBLISHED AS A **BOOK.**

 REALLY? HOW LONG WILL THAT TAKE?

 OH, ABOUT A WEEK.

 ONE WEEK LATER — HOW IS THE BOOK GOING, ROBIN?

 REALLY **BADLY,** THE CANADIAN PUBLISHING INDUSTRY IS **DEPRESSED** AND THE ONLY THINGS BEING PUBLISHED ARE **COOK BOOKS** AND **TRIVIA BOOKS**

 THAT'S **AWFUL!**

 OH, IT'S NOT SO BAD — I HAD THE IDEA TO **REWRITE** THESE STORIES AS A **COOKBOOK**

 IT WILL NEVER WORK

 ONLY, AS YOU KNOW, I **DON'T KNOW** HOW TO COOK

 ©

 ... SO I THOUGHT MAYBE **YOU** COULD **WRITE** THE **RECIPES**

 NO.

 WHY NOT?

 IT'S TOO MUCH **WORK**

 NO, IT'S **NOT**

 IT'S A **DUMB** IDEA

 **NO** IT'S **NOT**

 YES, IT **IS!**

 IS **NOT!**

 **IS!**

 **ISN'T!**

 **IS!**

 **ISN'T!**

 **IS** TO **INFINITY!**

 **ISN'T** TO INFINITY **PLUS 1!**

 I'M **RUBBER,** YOU'RE **GLUE.** WHATEVER YOU SAY **BOUNCES OFF** ME AND **STICKS** TO YOU!

 HEY, **WAIT A MINUTE,** PIERRE! THAT DOESN'T MAKE ANY SENSE... ... **ISN'T** TO INFINITY PLUS 1 BOUNCES OFF YOU AND STICKS TO ME... IT **DOESN'T WORK**

 YOU'LL HAVE TO THINK OF A **BETTER** RETORT

 NOW THAT THAT BOOK THING DIDN'T WORK WHAT ARE YOU GOING TO DO?

 WELL I ALWAYS WANTED TO **DRAW** SOME **COMICS,** SO I GUESS I'LL DO THAT

 CAN YOU MAKE **MONEY** WITH THAT?

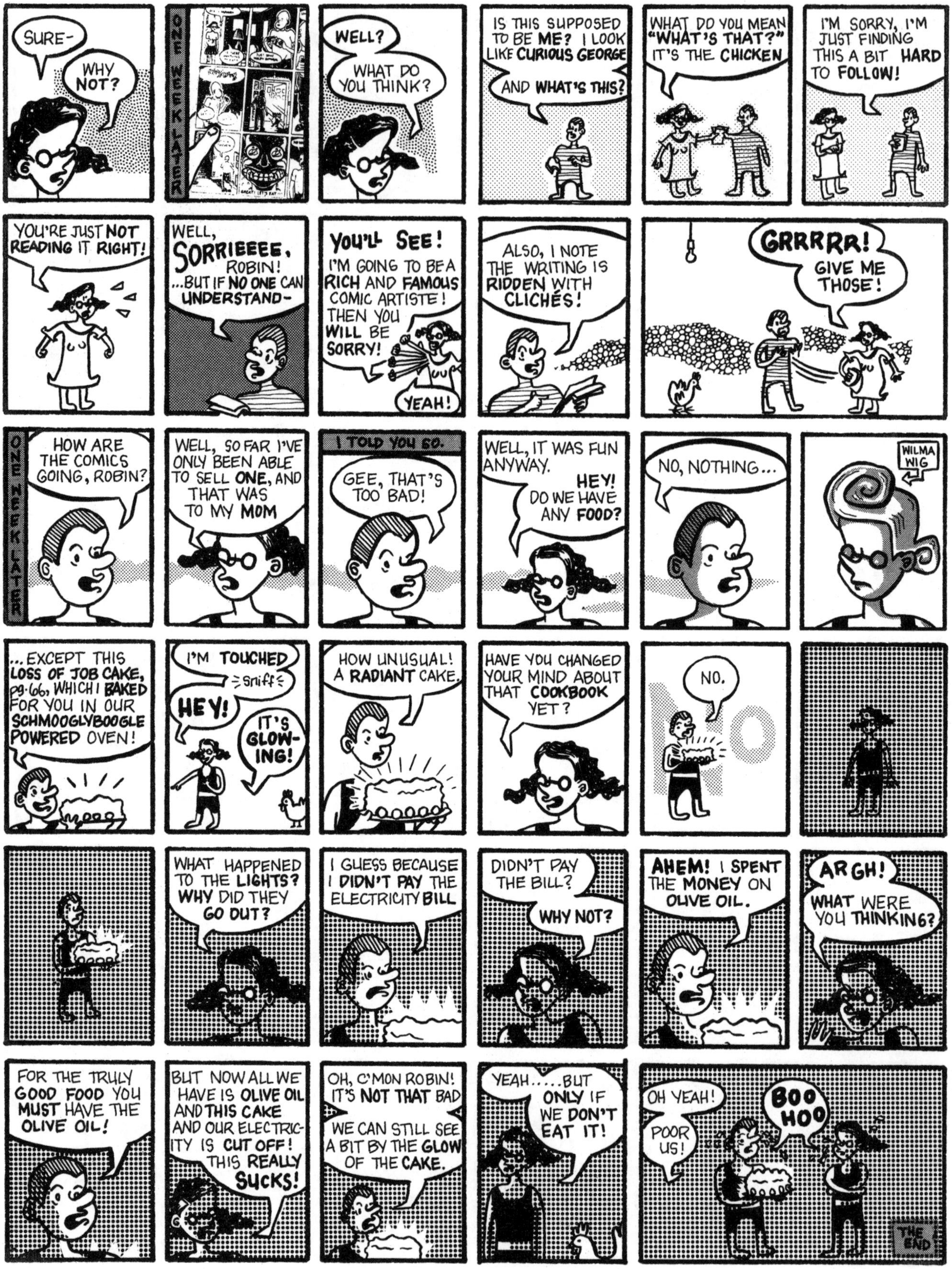
SURE-
WHY NOT?
ONE WEEK LATER
WELL?
WHAT DO YOU THINK?
IS THIS SUPPOSED TO BE ME? I LOOK LIKE CURIOUS GEORGE
AND WHAT'S THIS?
WHAT DO YOU MEAN "WHAT'S THAT?" IT'S THE CHICKEN
I'M SORRY, I'M JUST FINDING THIS A BIT HARD TO FOLLOW!
YOU'RE JUST NOT READING IT RIGHT!
WELL, SORRIEEEE, ROBIN! ...BUT IF NO ONE CAN UNDERSTAND-
YOU'LL SEE! I'M GOING TO BE A RICH AND FAMOUS COMIC ARTISTE! THEN YOU WILL BE SORRY!
YEAH!
ALSO, I NOTE THE WRITING IS RIDDEN WITH CLICHÉS!
GRRRRR! GIVE ME THOSE!
ONE WEEK LATER
HOW ARE THE COMICS GOING, ROBIN?
WELL, SO FAR I'VE ONLY BEEN ABLE TO SELL ONE, AND THAT WAS TO MY MOM
I TOLD YOU SO.
GEE, THAT'S TOO BAD!
WELL, IT WAS FUN ANYWAY.
HEY! DO WE HAVE ANY FOOD?
NO, NOTHING...
WILMA WIG
...EXCEPT THIS LOSS OF JOB CAKE, pg. 66, WHICH I BAKED FOR YOU IN OUR SCHMOOGLYBOOGLE POWERED OVEN!
I'M TOUCHED
sniff
HEY!
IT'S GLOWING!
HOW UNUSUAL! A RADIANT CAKE.
HAVE YOU CHANGED YOUR MIND ABOUT THAT COOKBOOK YET?
NO.
NO
WHAT HAPPENED TO THE LIGHTS? WHY DID THEY GO OUT?
I GUESS BECAUSE I DIDN'T PAY THE ELECTRICITY BILL
DIDN'T PAY THE BILL?
WHY NOT?
AHEM! I SPENT THE MONEY ON OLIVE OIL.
ARGH!
WHAT WERE YOU THINKING?
FOR THE TRULY GOOD FOOD YOU MUST HAVE THE OLIVE OIL!
BUT NOW ALL WE HAVE IS OLIVE OIL AND THIS CAKE AND OUR ELECTRICITY IS CUT OFF! THIS REALLY SUCKS!
OH, C'MON ROBIN! IT'S NOT THAT BAD
WE CAN STILL SEE A BIT BY THE GLOW OF THE CAKE.
YEAH.....BUT ONLY IF WE DON'T EAT IT!
OH YEAH!
POOR US!
BOO HOO
THE END

Basic Vegetable Broth

The Mother Juice.

10 cups cold water

2 carrots

2 onions

1 celery stalk

2 leeks

2 bunches green onion

1 parsnip, medium-sized

3 cloves garlic

1 tsp. thyme

2 bay leaves

1 small handful of parsley sprigs

3 tbsp. butter or oil (optional; see method 3 below)

salt and pepper (optional)

WASH ALL YOUR vegetables. Don't bother peeling them, not even the onions. But make sure you slice your leeks lengthwise and clean them because there is always dirt lodged between the layers. Cut everything into 1-inch cubes or so. You don't have to be too precise. Now you have 3 options:

1. Roll a big fatty and watch videos. Later on wallow in self-pity because you're hungry. Complain about the government.

2. Roll a big hootcher and set aside to smoke later. In a cast-iron skillet sauté the vegetables in the butter and a pinch of salt for 10 minutes. Chuck everything on the ingredient list into your stock pot with the sautéed vegetables.

3. Go cold turkey. Put all of the ingredients except the butter into the pot. This method is suggested for those watching their fat intake.

Now, for options 2 and 3 bring the broth to a slight boil and then reduce to a simmer for 60 to 90 minutes, then strain. Season to taste.

Makes 8 cups of broth.

COMPLEMENT WITH HERBS

Herbs are very effective in bringing up flavours that add dimension and depth to a recipe. The use of herbs is a very personal thing and should not be dictated, so in some ways this may be a breach of soup-making etiquette, but here are some handy hints on the making of broth.

Although the broth is generally the main ingredient of a soup in terms of quantity, it is not in terms of flavour. A broth should be relatively neutral. When making a broth, a proven basic of French cooking is to start with the thyme and bay leaf for a flavour-inducing stepping stone. Many herbs turn unsavoury after long periods of cooking, leaving you with the headache of masquerading their flavour and asking the burning question: "What happened?" As a rule of thumb, we use the more potent herbs in small quantities at the beginning of the broth-making and save the dominant flavours for the actual soup-making.

Variations

In lieu of giving a million recipes for vegetable broth—because we all know they exist—we're going to give you a few variations on the ones that we use. They fall into four basic categories:

The Heavy Root

The Basic Vegetable Broth recipe plus 2 extra carrots, 1 extra parsnip, 1 rutabaga, and 1/2 celeriac, and maybe 1 potato if you're feeling in a starchy mood (and maybe 1 lovage leaf, which is a parsley-family herb. We love lovage in this broth; when it cooks it just makes the whole room smell "HMMguh").

The Fun Guy

The Basic Vegetable Broth plus 2 cups of button mushrooms sautéed in a dry skillet for 5 minutes, a sprig of rosemary, and a small handful of dehydrated mushrooms (e.g., porcini, or morel; the flavour of a small amount will go a long way).

The Tangy

The Basic Vegetable Broth plus 3 tomatoes cut in quarters, 1/2 fennel, extra garlic, and a teaspoon of oregano. If you're really daring, you may want to add a whole hot pepper.

The Oriental

The Basic Vegetable Broth plus a chunk of ginger, 2 whole hot Asian chilies, and a few lime leaves. Add soy sauce to taste. Also, a splash of sherry is very effective.

Quiz for Unsure Broth Makers

Q: Can I use the strained vegetables from the broth?

A: Well, there are no laws prohibiting you from doing so, except for those governing good taste, but we strongly suggest you reserve them for your compost. They've rendered all their flavours and nutrients, and they will be like unidentifiable slime in your soup.

Q: Can I use dried-up broccoli in my broth?

A: No. The best way to make vegetable broth is by starting off with the freshest of ingredients. Sometimes back-of-the-fridge delights are not the way to go. Also, you should avoid certain vegetables when making broth: for example, broccoli, cauliflower, zucchini, bell peppers, and green beans. They can be best appreciated when used as a main ingredient of the soup.

Q: How about those bouillon cubes?

A: Many instant bouillons contain a high level of MSG and sodium, so if you really feel you must put some into the soup you have made from all fresh ingredients, select a brand that is free of MSG and low in sodium.

Q: What's so exciting about a bunch of vegetables, anyway?

A: Although vegetable broth is most commonly used in the preparation of soup, it is also a useful tool in vegetarian cooking, where the use of meat-based stocks is not at all acceptable. This is especially true for those on a no- or low-fat diet. So a big finger to those with the notion that meat stocks are the only way to add flavour to food.

STORING AND REHEATING SOUP

A soup should be thoroughly cooled before refrigerating. It will keep well in a sealed container for up to a week. If you're going to freeze the soup, might we suggest you portion it and freeze it on the day you make it or the day after.

Avoid the storage of soups containing milk products. They should be consumed the same day, or better yet, reserve the use of milk products until the soup gets to the dinner table and add them there.

When reheating a soup, ensure its temperature surpasses 150°. This is the temperature at which bacteria dies. Of course, most people don't have a thermometer in their kitchen, so try this: slowly reheat your soup and stir it until it comes to a slight boil. Stick your pinky finger into the soup pot. When it's too hot to stick your pinky into, it's ready (don't burn yourself).

Red Onion Soup

So good, it makes you cry.

6-8 cups cold water

5 red onions, sliced any way you want

3 tbsp. butter or oil

2 bay leaves

2 pinches of thyme, fresh or dry

splash of red wine (optional)

splash of soy sauce (optional)

salt and pepper to taste

IN A LARGE SOUP POT melt the butter over medium heat. Add the onions and a few pinches of salt. Reduce heat to low and cook for 30-60 minutes, stirring occasionally. The onions will begin to sweat and then will caramelize. Add the wine and stir in the thyme, water, bay leaves, and soy sauce (if desired).

Bring to a slight boil and let simmer uncovered for 40 minutes. Remove the bay leaves and adjust salt and pepper to taste.

Makes 4 hearty servings.

SERVING TIP

In the French tradition, Onion Soup is served in thick ceramic bowls. A chunk of French bread is ripped from the loaf by hand and placed on top of the soup, then the dish is generously sprinkled with grated Gruyère cheese and placed under the broiler until it is bubbly and golden brown. Topped with freshly chopped parsley.

Stinging Nettle Soup

At some New Age fat farms, nettles are used to slap your varicose veins. We prefer to eat them.

6-8 cups vegetable broth

1 large onion, finely diced

2 cups stinging nettle leaves, chopped into chiffonade

1 potato, cut into small cubes

2 bay leaves

3 tbsp. butter or oil

salt and pepper to taste

MELT THE BUTTER in the soup pot, then add the onions and salt and sauté for 3 minutes. Add the bay leaves, broth, and potato and bring to a boil. Keep it at a slight boil until the potato is starting to cook but still firm, about 5-10 minutes. Return it to a full boil and add the stinging nettle leaves. Reduce the heat to a simmer until the potato is completely cooked. Remove the bay leaves and season with salt and pepper to taste.

Makes 4 hearty servings.

A **STINGING NETTLE** IN SPRING

THE TRUTH ABOUT STINGING NETTLES

Stinging nettles grow in the wild and even around towns and cities, though we suggest you pick them where the soil is free from pollution. They act as a blood cleanser and contain a lot of iron; when cooked, they have a spinach-like flavour. They are covered with a fuzzy coat of fine needles that produce a burning sensation on your skin, so use scissors and wear rubber gloves any time you handle them. (These stingers "go away" during the cooking process.) They may be harvested throughout most of the year, depending on your local climate. They are most tender and sweet in early spring. Don't be a clear-cutting pig, just go for the leaves. When you get them home, pick out the stems and naughty bits, then wash them in cold water. You can blanch them, then use them as you would spinach. Save the blanching water for broth, or chill for iced stinging nettle tea. (Uncooked nettles can also be dried for tea.) Stinging nettles are not available at a store near you, except in some hippie markets.

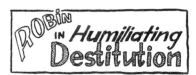

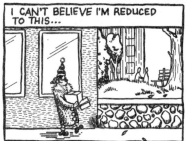

ROBIN IN Humiliating Destitution
I CAN'T BELIEVE I'M REDUCED TO THIS...
HOW HUMILIATING.
COMICS $2
STONER KITCHEN
I'M TOO EMBARRASSED TO SAY ANYTHING OR EVEN LOOK AT ANYBODY...
THOSE PEOPLE OVER THERE ARE LAUGHING AT ME!
SURE IS COLD.

THE DISCERNING PALATE

One day not long ago Pierre went to visit his friend Link Leisure, pop star, for a soup pot dinner for two. When Pierre arrived at Link's apartment, Link was in a state. He was trying on a "look" for an upcoming stage performance and had misplaced an element of his costume. Pierre asked Link what it was so he could assist him with the search. Link explained he had lost his prize prosthetic rubber pimple which he had purchased in London years ago and had never seen again for sale. "It's my lucky zit and I have to find it!" he insisted. He claimed he would be able to think of nothing else until the faux blemish had been found.

A meticulous and detailed search of the apartment failed to unearth the lucky prosthetic zit. It was the same colour as Link's carpet and about the size of a dime. Pierre was getting hungry and impatient. What was so urgent about a rubber zit? Eventually they gave up the hunt and decided to get stoned and eat together. Still in costume and consumed with thoughts of the zit, Link went to the kitchen and placed the soup pot to simmer.

Pierre turned the topic of conversation to Link's upcoming performance. As they discussed it, Pierre noted a strange, industrial odour had permeated the apartment, a smell not unlike a rotten cabbage burning. "I wish Link would remove the stock-making vegetables from his soup," thought Pierre. "That smell is so unappetizing."

"It's that new soup pot that Maria bought," said Link, referring to the unusual odour.

When the soup was served, Pierre blanched. What a stink! "But if I refuse to eat the soup, I will insult the cook," thought Pierre. "Most of my friends are reluctant to cook for me because with my superiorly refined palate they fear my criticisms. Since I don't want to create animosity I'll just eat this foul-smelling slop."

Pierre sat in paranoid silence, filling up on bread and hoping the flavour would grow on him. No such luck.

"May I have another glass of water?" asked Pierre.

"Sure," Link said, and went to the kitchen to get it. Coming back from the kitchen with the soup pot in his hands, he said to Pierre, "This soup is awful. I'm going to dump it."

"Well, now that you mention it I didn't like it either."

"I'm sorry. I'm going to the loo to give it the old flush-o-rama," said Link, as he headed for the bathroom.

Pierre heard a sudden shriek from Link. "Come quick, Pierre!"

In the bathroom he found Link standing over the toilet with the empty soup pot in his hands. "I found my zit!" he said tragically, and displayed the inside of the empty soup pot to Pierre. In the bottom remained the traces of the black burned rubber.

The lesson learned: keep track of your rubber zits while cooking.

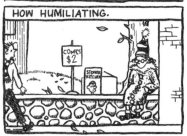

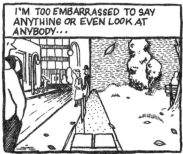

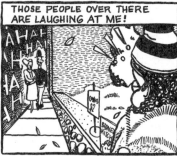

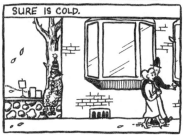

Potato Soup with Roasted Garlic and Onion

Asking yourself, "How can I make potatoes more glamourous?" Here's an idea!

6-8 cups vegetable broth

3-4 potatoes, cut into small cubes

1 large white onion, cut into quarters

2 whole bulbs of garlic

2 tbsp. olive oil (for roasting)

1 celery stalk, finely diced

1 bay leaf

1 tsp. thyme (optional)

2 tbsp. fresh parsley and/or a combination of herbs of your choice (e.g., chervil, rosemary, tarragon—all finely chopped)

salt and pepper to taste

START BY ROASTING the garlic and onion together with olive oil and a pinch of salt in a covered dish at 350° for 30-40 minutes. Let cool, then squish the pasty garlic cloves out of their skins. Then chop the onions in half and remove their skins.

In a soup pot put the broth, potatoes, celery, thyme, bay leaf, and salt. Bring it all to a boil, add the onions and garlic, then reduce to a simmer until the potatoes are fully cooked (about 25-30 minutes). Remove the bay leaf, add the fresh herbs, and adjust seasoning to taste. Quickly and coarsely purée, and you're done.

Nice with *crème fraîche* (pg. 50) or a splash of cream.

Makes 4 hearty servings.

Corn Chowder

Not mawkish or unsophisticated, as the use of the word "corn" implies.

CHOWDER CONSISTENCY

If you want your chowder to be thicker, take a potato masher to it, and mash about 25 percent of the total potato (it's hard to explain, but you understand this, right?).

BETH'S CHOWDER SECRET

Prepare the chowder in its entirety except for the milk and cilantro, then let it sit in the fridge overnight. The next day, reheat the chowder and add the milk and cilantro. This makes your chowder even more delicious than you ever thought possible, and will impress any lunch or dinner guest.

4 cups vegetable broth

2 potatoes, diced into small cubes

1 onion, diced

2 cloves of garlic, minced

3 tbsp. flour

3 tbsp. butter

1 cup whole kernel corn, fresh, frozen, or canned

2 cups puréed corn or a large tin of creamed corn

2 yellow peppers, charred, seeded, skinned, and diced (see method, pg. 74—optional)

1 tsp. thyme

1 bay leaf

pinch of cumin

1 cup milk or cream

1 tbsp. fresh cilantro leaves, finely chopped

salt and pepper to taste

IN A LARGE SOUP POT over medium heat, melt the butter and add the onions and garlic with a pinch of salt. Sauté for 3 minutes. Reduce the heat to low and stir in the flour and cumin. Let cook for 5 minutes, stirring enough not to burn it all, and to permit even cooking of ingredients.

Meanwhile in a separate pot, boil the potatoes until they are almost cooked but still quite firm. Discard the water but do not rinse the potatoes.

Back to the soup pot: stir in the puréed corn and broth until you have a smooth, even texture. Crank up the heat to high. Add the thyme and bay leaf, corn, potatoes, and optional roasted yellow bell peppers. Bring to a slight boil, reduce the heat, and let simmer for 10 minutes. Remove the bay leaf. Add the milk and the cilantro before serving, and season to taste.

Makes 6-8 servings.

Tomato Soup

Here's a recipe for an old standby. But watch out: if you eat the seeds from a tomato, a plant will grow out of your ass!

2 cups vegetable broth or water

8-12 fresh roma tomatoes, skinned, seeded, and quartered
  (see pg. 11)

1 large onion, finely diced

3 cloves garlic, minced

2 tbsp. olive oil (or fat of your choice)

1/2 tbsp. oregano

1 tbsp. freshly chopped parsley

2 tbsp. fresh basil leaves, cut into chiffonade

pinch of cayenne pepper

1 tbsp. brown sugar (optional)

salt and pepper to taste

IN YOUR SOUP POT, heat the oil over medium high heat. Add the onion and salt and sauté for 3 minutes. Stir in the garlic, oregano, and cayenne pepper and cook for another 3 minutes. If you are using sugar, add it before the next step, which is adding the broth and tomatoes. Bring it to a slight boil, then stir in the parsley. Reduce the heat and simmer for 25 minutes. Add the basil and simmer for another 5 minutes. Adjust seasoning to taste, then purée.

Delicious with *crème fraîche* (pg. 50) or sour cream.

Makes 4-6 servings.

SUBLIMINAL ALPHABET SOUP FOR DATES

① DECIDE WHAT SORT OF **SUBLIMINAL MESSAGE** YOU'D LIKE TO **SEND** TO YOUR **DATE**

A:

② GO TO THE BULK STORE AND BUY BULK **ALPHABET PASTA**. LATER AT HOME PICK OUT THE **LETTERS** THAT **SPELL** YOUR **MESSAGE**.

B:

③ ADD TO **TOMATO SOUP**

C:

④ SERVE TO DATE

GUARANTEED RESULTS!

A: SEX B: EAT ME C: I'M LEAVING YOU

I'M RICH!

SUDDENLY IT'S SPRING

I'M BEAUTIFUL!

Wow! Big head!

SHOVE!

Get out of my way, Bub!

POEMS $2

I'M TALENTED!

Wait! On second thought, please accept this large bag of money!

HOT DIGGETY DOG!

BUT WHAT'S THIS? WE LAST LEFT OUR HEROINE COLD AND BEGGARED ON A STOOP, SORT OF LIKE 'THE LITTLE MATCH GIRL', SO WHAT CURIOUS TURN OF EVENTS COULD ELEVATE HER TO THIS STATE OF SELF CONGRATULATORY BLISS? AND WHAT DOES THIS HAVE TO DO WITH FOOD?*

I'M RICH!

Now that I'm wealthy I can afford to be nice!

ZOOM

SPARE CHANGE

STONER POETRY

*NOTHING.

Baba Stoyko's Beet Borsch

A hearty soup to make you want to dance naked in the snow.

4 cups water

4-6 fresh beets

3 cloves garlic, minced

1 large onion, diced

1 celery stalk, finely diced, including the small tender leaves

2 cups red cabbage, shredded

2-3 potatoes, diced

1 cup parsnip, or combination of root vegetables, diced

1 cup stewed tomatoes

1 cup cooked broad beans

2 tbsp. oil or butter

1 tbsp. dill seed

2 tbsp. fresh chopped dill (dry will also do)

juice of 1 lemon

1 bay leaf

dash of apple cider vinegar (optional)

salt and pepper to taste

CUT 4 OR 5 OF THE BEETS into stick-like shapes (the proper cooking term is *bâtons*). Grate the remaining beets into a bowl, then add the lemon juice and the bâtons of beet and reserve.

In a large soup pot over medium heat sauté the onions and garlic in oil with a pinch of salt for 3 minutes. Stir in the cabbage, celery, and dill seeds, then sauté for a few minutes more. Add the broth, and dump in the bowl of beets, including the liquid. Bring to a slight boil and then add the remaining ingredients except the chopped dill. When all returns to a slight boil, reduce to a simmer for 40 to 60 minutes. Remove the bay leaf. Stir in the fresh dill and adjust seasonings to taste.

Serve topped with plain yoghurt or sour cream.

Makes 8 servings.

POSSIBLE SIDE EFFECTS OF BABA STOYKO'S BEET BORSCH ON THE UNSUSPECTING

Years after Baba Stoyko's death, we went to her granddaughter's Ukrainian Christmas party. Ukrainian Christmas happens in January, in case you don't know, and this year it fell on a very snowy day of the type that people claim to hate but secretly love. Although such days in Vancouver rarely occur, and the city was half shut-down, most of the invited guests managed to make it to the party because everyone loves a Ukrainian Christmas.

Much care was taken to make the Christmas party as Ukrainian as possible. There were the Ukrainian treats—including, of course, perogies and Baba Stoyko's infamous Beet Borsch—and there was also a not-quite-understood Mexican sweet loaf with a plastic baby in it thrown in for cheap exoticism. To help create the right party atmosphere, a vinyl recording of the Balkan Women's Choir was playing on the turntable. Following Ukrainian Christmas tradition, everyone drank large quantities of Eastern European moonshine, so they were rather relaxed and loose when the pot of Baba Stoyko's Beet Borsch was finally presented with much fanfare.

The heavenly aroma was like another living entity entering the room, filled with personality and promise and capturing everyone's rapt attention. Social conventions were ignored as people gathered in a tight knot around the pot, so eager were they to taste such soup. Within a few minutes the pot was empty and stomachs were full.

"Suddenly and for no explained reason I feel like jumping around naked in the snow," said Cathy, the hostess.

"That's strange. So do I!" said all the guests in unison.

Cathy quickly made a couple of kerosene-soaked cloth torches while guests scrambled to find their footwear. A mountain of party clothes was heaped near the door and everyone ran out in the yard.

"Let's build an igloo thingy!"

"No. Let's make snow angels."

"No. Let's make a snowman!"

"No. Let's go back inside. I'm freezing!"

Everyone agreed with the last sentiment and ran back into the house for more moonshine. They had only been out for about forty-five seconds, but you know, with all these buildings with central heating, Northerners just aren't that hardy anymore.

When asked later by disconcerted neighbours to explain the bizarre behaviour of her party guests, Cathy could only reply, "It must have been something they ate."

So if you plan to serve Baba Stoyko's Beet Borsch to anyone, think first about whether you want to see that person jump around naked in your backyard for forty-five seconds. If your answer is "no," we suggest you peruse this book for an alternative savoury soup recipe. If it is "yes," go for it.

CRÈME FRAÎCHE

It's chi-chi sour cream.

3/4 cup whipping cream

1/4 cup buttermilk or sour
  cream

Combine all the ingredients
and leave in an airtight
container at room
temperature overnight, or at
least 12 hours. For thicker
crème fraîche, leave out for
longer. This will keep for
about two weeks in an
airtight container in your
fridge.

Makes 1 cup.

Roasted Pumpkin Soup with Coconut Milk

There are few things we crave on a cold day. This is one of them.

4 cups vegetable broth

2 cups roasted pumpkin, pg. 51

1 8 oz. can coconut milk

1/2 cup tomato concassé

2 tbsp. kecap manis (sweet soy sauce)

chunk of fresh ginger the size of a tbsp.

2 lime leaves or 1 slice lime rind

1 hot Asian pepper, whole

salt and pepper to taste

FIRST, PREPARE the roasted pumpkin. Then, in a large soup pot at
high heat add the broth, the chunk of ginger, the whole Asian
pepper, and the lime leaves. Bring to a slight boil and let simmer
for at least 20 minutes. Purée the roasted pumpkin flesh and
coconut milk in the food processor (this can also be done by hand
with a potato masher). Remove the ginger, pepper, and lime leaves
from the broth and discard. Stir the pumpkin coconut milk mush
into the broth with the kecap manis and the tomato concassé. Stir
well and season to taste.

Serve with a dollop of *crème fraîche*, or fresh Thai basil or chives.

Makes 4-6 servings.

Roasted Pumpkin for Soup

This also tastes great simply as a side dish.

2 medium-sized chunks of pumpkin, skin on, seeds out

2 large cloves garlic, skinned and slivered

2 tbsp. olive oil

2 tsp. palm sugar (or brown sugar; don't use honey, it burns)

1/4 tsp. speculaas spice mix

salt and pepper to taste

PREHEAT OVEN to 350°.

With a knife make some incisions into the flesh side of the pumpkin and insert the garlic slivers into them. Sprinkle the speculaas spice, palm sugar, and salt and pepper onto the pumpkin flesh. Rub the olive oil all over the flesh (ooh, baby!). Place the pumpkin flesh side down onto a baking dish and roast covered for 30-40 minutes, or until the flesh is tender.

Let cool, then scoop out the flesh and juices.

Makes about 2 cups.

SPECULAAS

You can buy speculaas at a Dutch deli if you have one in your town; otherwise try a gourmet spice store. This spice was named after St. Nicholas of Myra (speculaas means "speculator," which was his job with the church), and is strongly associated with Christmas baking in the Netherlands. It is composed of equal parts of ground ginger, cinnamon, cardomon, cloves, and white pepper.

Gazpacho Andaluz

There are few things we crave on a hot day. This is one of them.

2 cups water or V8 juice

6 tomatoes, cut in quarters

1 cucumber, partially peeled, cut in large chunks and seeded (save the juice)

1 green pepper, cut in half and seeded

4-6 cloves garlic, crushed

1 1/2 cups bread scraps

4 tbsp. parsley, coarsely chopped

dash of hot chili sauce

drizzle of fine olive oil

1/2 tsp. cayenne pepper

salt and pepper to taste

splash of sherry wine vinegar

1 cup ice cubes

THROW IT ALL in the blender or food processor. (A food mill or a hand grater will do the trick if you don't have a food processor. Or maybe your friend or neighbour will lend you one. Or then again, ask a cherished family member to buy you one as a gift.) Purée. Adjust seasoning to taste. Let chill for at least an hour.

Makes 4 hearty servings.

HOT GARDEN TIPS

A few years ago, Pierre visited his friend Omar, who was living on a farm in northern Spain. He had a lush and productive vegetable garden happening there which Pierre enjoyed working in and cooking from. One day, they had an over-the-fence chat with a neighbouring woman. She was an older, small-in-stature Catalonian who spoke not a word of English. Their conversation was basic and broken, for Omar spoke only a bit of textbook Spanish, and Pierre none at all (except for a few cooking terms).

Somehow Omar and the neighbour managed a conversation about his garden. The woman was impressed by its healthy virility and desired to know the secret of Omar's green thumb. Omar said, "I use the *verduras* (vegetables)." He explained the concept of composting to her as well as he could with the language limitations they shared. She seemed to understand and left happy and anxious to try it.

The next morning Omar and Pierre were wakened from their sleep by an insistent pounding on the front door. It was the Catalonian neighbour, who was displaying an irateness so acute some might describe it as rabid anger. With a barrage of unintelligible Spanish and exaggerated gestures, she made the two men understand to follow her to her garden. They arrived to see row upon row of dead plants with steaming vegetables amidst them. The woman picked an empty soup pot from the ground and waved it over her head and, shaking her other fist angrily, delivered a persistent and virulent monologue about foreigners to the two friends.

"I think I understand," said Pierre to Omar. "This woman has poured hot vegetable broth onto her plants, thereby inadvertently killing them. She must have misunderstood about the compost."

Not knowing what else to do, they turned their back on the still deafeningly vocal woman and headed back to Omar's farm.

"She might just be stupid," said Omar. "She and her husband are both under four feet tall, and when I told them how the lead pipe water system they have here can stunt growth they said, `It never affected us.'"

"It's weird they don't know about compost, though," Pierre said.

"Yeah, it is weird."

"Maybe you should practice your Spanish more."

"Yeah."

But he moved away instead.

Fresh Pea Soup with Tempeh

We traded this with Robin's brother Adam, who lives in North Carolina, in exchange for the head of Jesse Helms. But when the head arrived in the mail, it had transformed into a newspaper clipping.

4-6 cups Oriental broth, pg. 40

3 cups peas, fresh or frozen

1 onion finely chopped

1 celery stalk, finely chopped

1 tsp. thyme

pinch of speculaas (or 5-spice or nutmeg)

1 bay leaf

1 tbsp. any kind of cooking oil

3 tbsp. butter

3 tbsp. flour

2 tbsp. miso

salt and pepper to taste

IN A SOUP POT, sauté the onions and celery with a pinch of salt in the any-kind-of cooking oil for 3 minutes. Add the broth, bay leaf, thyme, and speculaas and bring to a slight boil. Add the peas and reduce to simmer for 10 minutes or until the peas are completely cooked but still bright green.

Meanwhile, heat a skillet to medium heat and thoroughly melt the butter in it, then remove it from the heat. Sift in the flour and mix in well with a wooden spoon. Return to a very low heat and let it cook 3-5 minutes, gently stirring occasionally to avoid burning. (This is a brown roux, pg. 8.) Remove the skillet from the stove and let the roux cool, then stir in the miso with a wooden spoon (see note).

Stir the roux into the soup and let it simmer at a very low heat for another 5 minutes. Remove the bay leaf and season to taste.

Purée and strain. Get those icky pea skins out.

Stir in Tempeh cubes before serving.

Makes 4-6 servings.

MISO WARNING

Never boil Miso. Ya kill it!

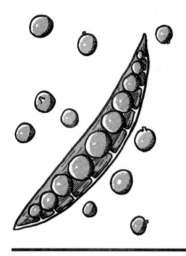

TEMPEH CUBES

1 block tempeh

1/4 cup oil

pinch of salt

Chop the tempeh into 1/8-inch cubes. In a cast-iron skillet, heat the oil over medium high heat, then fry the tempeh cubes with the salt for about 5 minutes or until they are golden brown. When they are done, blot them on some paper towels or a brown paper bag.

Mushroom Soup

One of the more controversial recipes in the book.

4 cups vegetable broth

1 pound button mushrooms, sliced

1 large onion, diced

2 tbsp. butter

1/4 cup flour

1 bay leaf

1 tbsp. leaf parsley, finely chopped

1 tsp. fresh rosemary, finely chopped

1/2 tsp. thyme, finely chopped

splash of wine (optional)

1/2 cup heavy cream

salt and pepper to taste

IN A LARGE SKILLET over high heat, melt the butter and add the onion and a pinch of salt. Sauté for 3 minutes. Add the mushrooms, rosemary, thyme, and optional wine, and sauté for another 3 minutes. Sift in flour and stir well with a wooden spoon to avoid lumps. Reduce heat to low and let it cook for another 5 minutes, stirring occasionally.

Pour the vegetable broth into a soup pot and add the sautéed mushrooms. Use a half cup of broth to deglaze the skillet and add it to the soup pot. Add the parsley and simmer for 20 minutes.

Remove the bay leaf, pour in cream, season to taste and serve.

Makes 4-6 servings.

PIERRE! I'M HOME!

HOW DID THE COMIC SELLING GO, ROBIN?

REALLY WELL! I'M FABULOUSLY RICH NOW! AND I'M PROBABLY GOING TO BE FAMOUS, TOO!

WOW! EVERYONE LOVED YOUR COMICS!

WELL, NOT EXACTLY...

DID A LOT OF PEOPLE LOOK?

UH... NO.

HOW MANY PEOPLE LOOKED?

2 PEOPLE LOOKED

HEY! THE LIGHTS ARE ON!

YES. I PAID THE ELECTRICAL BILL

WHOOOiiiiE! NOW WE CAN EAT THIS CAKE!

PIERRE! HOW CAN YOUR ATTENTION WANDER WHEN I'M TELLING YOU HOW I CAME TO BE FABULOUSLY RICH?

SORRY, ROBIN. SO, 2 PEOPLE LOOKED AND BOUGHT THEM ALL?

NOT EXACTLY

I GOT SCARED AND RAN AWAY, THEN I BURNED MOST OF THE COMICS TO STAY WARM. IT WAS COLD AND I COULDN'T GET ANYONE TO LOOK AT THE COMICS AND I FELT REALLY PARANOID. THEN I FELL TO SLEEP.

AND YOU WOKE UP FABULOUSLY RICH!

SORT OF

WHAT DO YOU MEAN "SORT OF"?

I WOKE UP AND SOME GUY WAS READING MY COMIC BOOK...

HE WAS LAUGHING AND LAUGHING...

HAHA HAR HELL NO MASSACHUSETTS ANYONE?
Ho! IS YLE 6 SNORK
7 ATE 9
HAR!
RUN JIM!
SNERK
DANDY CANDY
SAVE THE STAMPS!
FREE RANGE EGGS STONER KIT COMICS $2 CITY FRESH

HE CONVINCED ME I AM BRILLIANT, BEAUTIFUL AND TALENTED, AND THEN BOUGHT THE RIGHTS TO THE COMICS WITH THESE BAGS OF MONEY

HEP HAR
THRILL BRILL BRILLIANT QUADRILLE
WHAT ABOUT HER? SHE'S GOOD LOOKING
I SAID RUN JIM HAR HR
HA
GALLANT TALL ANT TALENT
Thank you! I know!

HE SAID HE'S GOING TO PRINT IT AND MAIL COPIES TO INFLUENTIAL PEOPLE HE KNOWS...

HE LEFT BEFORE I REALLY WOKE UP

YEP I ATE THE CAK
Har!
Hey y Get J Jell
Who was that plainly insane man?

CAN THAT MAKE YOU FAMOUS?

I THINK SO... ANYWAY, HE BOUGHT THE LAST UNBURNED COPY SO AFTER THAT I CAME HOME.

IS THAT A **TRUE** STORY?

YES

ARE YOU **SURE** YOU DIDN'T MAKE THAT UP? I MEAN, IT'S **TOO** CHEESY!

TOO CHEESY BUT **TRUE.** LOOK AT THESE **BAGS** OF **MONEY.** I SWEAR IT'S ALL TRUE.

I SWEAR!

IS THAT WHEN YOUR HEAD GOT SO **UNUSUALLY LARGE?**

YES. I DISCOVERED MY **INNER PRINCESS!**

HOO BOY

YOU LOOK MORE LIKE A **DEFORMED CIRCUS FREAK!**

HAR!

WHY, **THANKS, PIERRE!** DON'T FORGET I'M A **WEALTHY PRINCESS** NOW!

I **MEANT** TO SAY YOU LOOK 'REGAL' HAVE SOME CAKE

I WISH IT WASN'T **ILLEGAL** TO QUIT YOUR **JOB.** THEN I COULD LEAVE 'TOAST 'R' US'

MAYBE YOU COULD **ARRANGE** TO GET "FIRED"

AND **YOU CAN SUPPORT ME** WITH YOUR COMICS.

NAH, I'M NOT GOING TO MAKE ANYMORE.

WHY?

IT'S GOING SO **WELL.**

AW, **FACE IT, PIERRE!** THAT WAS A 'ONCE IN A LIFETIME' FLUKE!

IF AT FIRST YOU DON'T SUCCEED, **GIVE UP!**

THIS EXPERIENCE TAUGHT ME THAT PEOPLE **DON'T CARE** ABOUT COMICS AND **POVERTY** TRULY DOES **SUCK.** IF I CAN'T GET **INSTANT** RECOGNITION, REMUNERATION AND APPROVAL FROM THE COMMON MASSES TO **VALIDATE MYSELF** AND WHAT I DO IT'S **JUST NOT WORTH IT!**

WELL, WHAT ARE YOU GOING TO DO **NOW,** THEN?

EAT, GET **HIGH,** AND WATCH T.V.

I FEEL LIKE SOMETHING'S NOT **QUITE** RIGHT

ME TOO

I THINK IT'S ALL THIS **MONEY.** IT'S SHAKEN MY **SENSE** OF **IDENTITY!**

MAYBE WE SHOULD **SPEND** IT

WE SHOULD AT LEAST HAVE AN **EXTRAVAGANT** PARTY! A **DELUXE DINNER** PARTY WITH THE MOST **SPARKLING** OF GUESTS!

Eiiilg!

WHAT?

I JUST **STEPPED** ON A **RAW EGG!**

HA HA

LET'S MAKE THAT CHICKEN **LEAVE**

YOU KNOW, TODAY I HAD A 99¢ SLICE OF PIZZA (SPICY VEGE-TARIAN) AND I WAS **DEPRESSED** BECAUSE ALL I COULD **AFFORD** TO **EAT** WAS THE PIZZA, AND I WAS LOOKING AT IT AND **JONI MITCH-ELL** APPEARED ON THE **PIZZA!**

YOU SAW AN **APPARITION** OF **JONI MITCHELL** ON YOUR 99¢ **PIZZA SLICE?!**

YEAH, AND I WAS INSTANTLY FILLED WITH THIS **FEEL-ING** THAT WAS LIKE A **DAZZ-LING BLUE LIGHT!** ...IF YOU COULD **FEEL LIGHT,** I MEAN

WHAT?

AND EVER SINCE THEN I'VE BEEN **HAPPY!**

IS THAT **TRUE?**

NO

I MADE IT UP

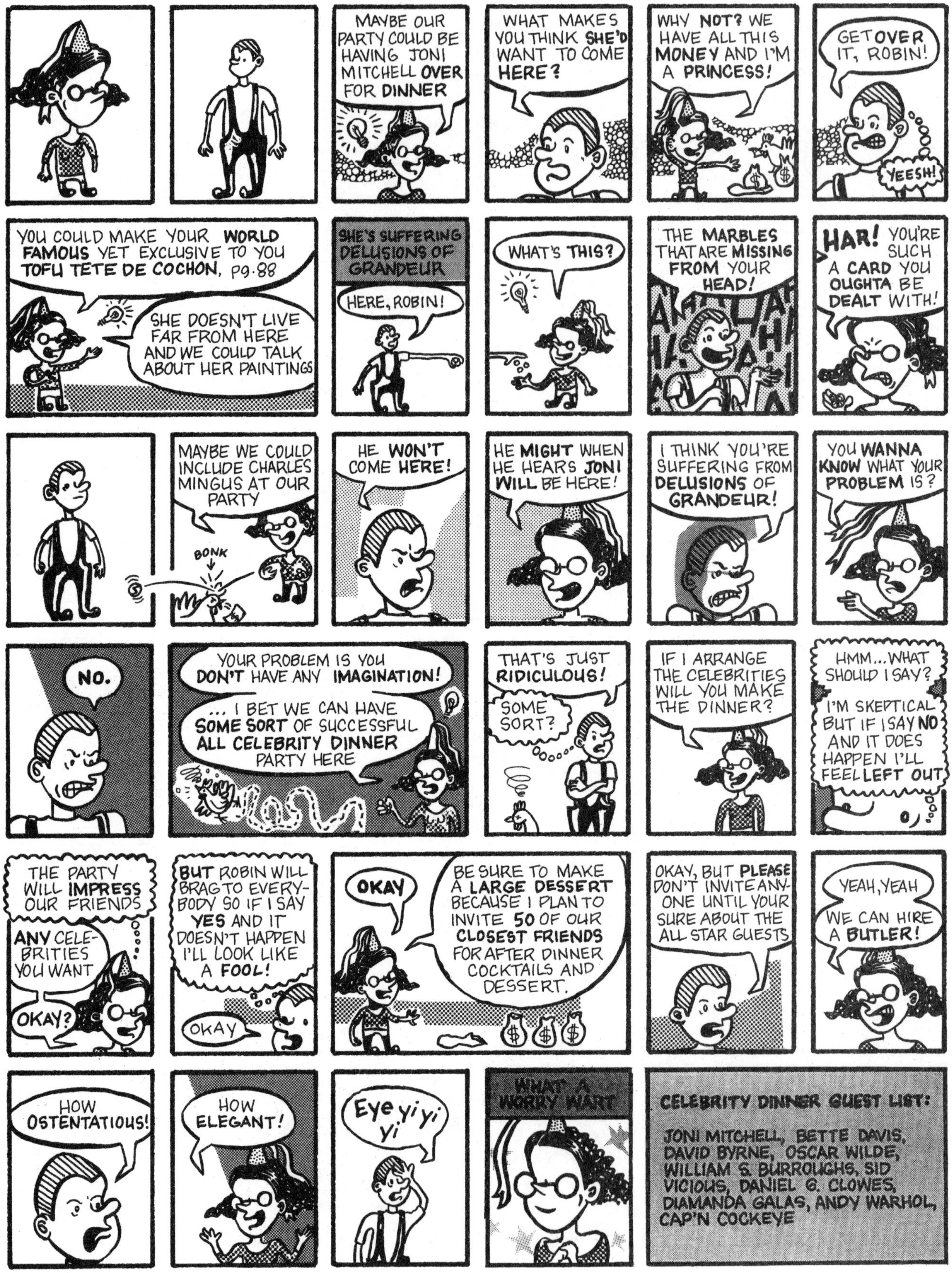

MAYBE OUR PARTY COULD BE HAVING JONI MITCHELL OVER FOR DINNER
WHAT MAKES YOU THINK SHE'D WANT TO COME HERE?
WHY NOT? WE HAVE ALL THIS MONEY AND I'M A PRINCESS!
GET OVER IT, ROBIN!
YEESH!
YOU COULD MAKE YOUR WORLD FAMOUS YET EXCLUSIVE TO YOU TOFU TETE DE COCHON, pg. 88
SHE DOESN'T LIVE FAR FROM HERE AND WE COULD TALK ABOUT HER PAINTINGS
SHE'S SUFFERING DELUSIONS OF GRANDEUR
HERE, ROBIN!
WHAT'S THIS?
THE MARBLES THAT ARE MISSING FROM YOUR HEAD!
HAR! YOU'RE SUCH A CARD YOU OUGHTA BE DEALT WITH!
MAYBE WE COULD INCLUDE CHARLES MINGUS AT OUR PARTY
BONK
HE WON'T COME HERE!
HE MIGHT WHEN HE HEARS JONI WILL BE HERE!
I THINK YOU'RE SUFFERING FROM DELUSIONS OF GRANDEUR!
YOU WANNA KNOW WHAT YOUR PROBLEM IS?
NO.
YOUR PROBLEM IS YOU DON'T HAVE ANY IMAGINATION!
... I BET WE CAN HAVE SOME SORT OF SUCCESSFUL ALL CELEBRITY DINNER PARTY HERE
THAT'S JUST RIDICULOUS!
SOME SORT?
IF I ARRANGE THE CELEBRITIES WILL YOU MAKE THE DINNER?
HMM... WHAT SHOULD I SAY?
I'M SKEPTICAL BUT IF I SAY NO AND IT DOES HAPPEN I'LL FEEL LEFT OUT
THE PARTY WILL IMPRESS OUR FRIENDS
ANY CELEBRITIES YOU WANT
OKAY?
BUT ROBIN WILL BRAG TO EVERYBODY SO IF I SAY YES AND IT DOESN'T HAPPEN I'LL LOOK LIKE A FOOL!
OKAY
OKAY
BE SURE TO MAKE A LARGE DESSERT BECAUSE I PLAN TO INVITE 50 OF OUR CLOSEST FRIENDS FOR AFTER DINNER COCKTAILS AND DESSERT.
OKAY, BUT PLEASE DON'T INVITE ANYONE UNTIL YOUR SURE ABOUT THE ALL STAR GUESTS
YEAH, YEAH
WE CAN HIRE A BUTLER!
HOW OSTENTATIOUS!
HOW ELEGANT!
Eye yi yi yi
WHAT A WORRY WART
CELEBRITY DINNER GUEST LIST:
JONI MITCHELL, BETTE DAVIS, DAVID BYRNE, OSCAR WILDE, WILLIAM S. BURROUGHS, SID VICIOUS, DANIEL G. CLOWES, DIAMANDA GALAS, ANDY WARHOL, CAP'N COCKEYE

Party!

A party can be as simple as filling the tub with ice and beer, but like many things in life, the more you put into it the more you get out of it, so we like to use a little imagination for our party agendas.

One time Robin arranged her own surprise birthday party, complete with games and prizes. "I never got so many presents before," said the radiant birthday girl. "I really cleaned up." Other past party adventures we got caught up in include an indoor roller blade derby, cheesy Dutch karaoke, impromptu lip-synch contests, and a tribute to Dr. Seuss (the party-wear seen at this one was phenomenal). We can't really remember them all 'cause it's just a big blur, but we had fun.

Even if the ideas mentioned here aren't really your style, the possibilities are endless. We're sure you can come up with themes to suit you that will be equally entertaining. Don't be lazy now, and remember: It's a party, not a *bored* meeting.

Emily Stewart, Martha Crocker, Betty Post, and You

Hostess WITH THE mostess

YOUR NAME HERE

A party is an involved project. First, brainstorm on what you will make for dinner. Consider your own cooking abilities, the likes and dislikes of your guests, the season and the mood you want to set, and also the amount of time and money you can afford to spend on your preparations. Prepare food that is simple yet elegant (save the risotto sushi rolls with Cajun peanut sauce for people you hate). Only the foolishly brave will attempt to prepare a complicated dish they've never made before and serve it to guests. Also, if you are serving a multi-course meal, it is important that you don't repeat the same main ingredient in different courses (for instance, tomato soup, then tomato salad, then tomato sauce).

Once you've completed your menu, break it down to a list of ingredients you will need, then check to see what you have in stock and what you will need to buy.

Be organized. It's easier to prepare a menu step by step starting days ahead rather than trying to do everything on the day of the party.

Let us take you through the process of preparing the food for a party. Follow us to our *Scrambled Brains* Laboratory, where you will prepare the meal for our all-celebrity dinner.

MENU:

Soup	Stinging Nettle Soup, pg. 43
Salad	Roasted Oyster Mushroom and Bocconcini Salad, pg. 82
Appetizer	Hell Turds with lemon yoghurt and salted cucumbers, pg. 84
Entrée	*Tofu Tête de Cochon*, pg. 88, *à la jardinière*
Dessert	Aunt Agnes' 12 Layer Cake, pg. 66

This party menu, designed for approximately 8 guests, will take 4 days' work, but will also permit you to entertain your guests in a relaxed atmosphere, and that, my dears, is the cat's meow.

Day 1: The first day will be devoted to Aunt Agnes. Follow the recipe for Basic Chocolate Cake, pg. 64, and repeat 6 times for 12 cakes. When the cakes have all cooled, wrap them in cellophane and put them in the freezer to be taken out the night before the "do."

Day 2: Go to the store and buy everything you will need on your grocery list except for the salad greens and mushrooms. (Remember, the fresher your ingredients are, the better your party will be, and you will be crowned the hostess with the mostess, all because you bought your greens at the last minute.) This day is also good for a range of other hostess duties such as confirming your guest list, housecleaning, rearranging your furniture, and practicing stimulating chit-chat in front of the mirror. Don't forget to presoak the garbanzo beans for your Hell Turds. Get to bed early, there's a big cooking day ahead.

Day 3: With your morning coffee in hand, write up a prep list of all the things you have to make. When you have completed each dish, give yourself a gold star. Prepare the Stinging Nettle Soup but exclude the stinging nettle. Let cool and refrigerate. Prepare the Hell Turd mixture but do not form into balls. Refrigerate in a sealed container. Also prepare the salted cucumbers, to be served with the Hell Turds. Prepare the *Tofu Tête de Cochon*, but do not bake. Refrigerate. Take the 12 cakes from the freezer and leave them out to defrost.

Day 4: Wake up exhausted and slightly sick. Suddenly realize you forgot to stock up at the liquor store. Get out the granny shopping cart and head on down. On the way, stop in an open field and pick some dandelion greens for your salad. Take out your rubber gloves and get your stinging nettles. Also, stop at the produce store for more salad greens and mushrooms. Hurry home after you've visited the liquor store as this is your last chance to clean the house. Why didn't you do it on Day 2 as we suggested?

Crack open a beer and don that little plaid apron. Okay, here we go:

MULTIPLY the Butter Icing recipe, pg. 65, by 6 and make it.

CONSTRUCT Aunt Agnes' 12 Layer Cake. (It is recommended you skip the Rumball-eating process during this time.)

PREPARE the Oyster Mushroom Salad, but don't broil the mushrooms yet.

CLEAN the stinging nettles and prepare them for the soup. Don't add them to the soup until the soup is heated and almost ready to serve, which of course is later on.

CHEEZIE INSIGHT

Wracking your brain for a new way to serve Cheezies? Try offering them on bamboo skewers. And at Easter time, arrange them in a cross pattern.

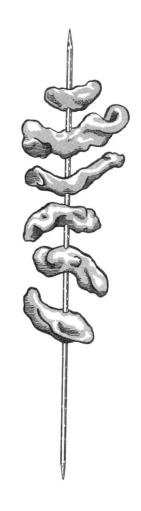

WASH all the salad greens and put them in the fridge to chill. You can also clean and chop some vegetables to be served with the *Tofu Tête de Cochon.*

ROLL out the Hell Turds and brown them (1 minute on each side), to be reheated right before serving. Please note that usually you don't cook the Turds twice, but in this case it is better because of time considerations.

PREPARE the Lemon Yoghurt.

BAKE the *Tofu Tête de Cochon* about an hour before you think you will serve the Warm Oyster Mushroom salad (it takes about 50 minutes to bake).

CHANGE into your party clothes. If you're anything like us, you have planned your "kit" far in advance, so slip that on and await your guests.

RETURN to the kitchen about half an hour before it's time to eat.

PLACE your soup pot to simmer. Bring it to a boil and add the stinging nettles.

SEAT your guests. Have your butler serve the soup. If you do not have a butler, as the hostess it is your misfortune to have to:

LEAVE the table in the middle of the soup course and remove the *Tofu Tête de Cochon* from the oven and wrap it in foil. Roast the oyster mushrooms for the salad, carefully and religiously following the complete instructions on pg. 82.

TURN down the oven to 350° and return to the table to remove the soup bowls and replace them with plates of salad. Sit down and eat your salad really quickly, then run back into the kitchen and throw the Turds in the oven, unless you haven't completely lost it by now, in which case you will place them on a baking sheet *before* tossing them into the oven.

PREPARE the plates while your Turds are in the oven (see pg. 85). Also boil some water for the steamed seasonal vegetables.

REMOVE the salad plates from the table and replace them with plates of Hell Turds. Refuse all offers of help, no matter how sincere. Respond to all compliments with phrases such as, "Oh, it was nothing. I just whipped it together in my spare time. I got the recipe from *Scrambled Brains*. Do you have a copy yet? I highly recommend you get one."

RETURN to the kitchen. Pause for a moment to have a nip on that bottle of scotch you hid under the sink. Put the vegetables on to steam. Garnish the *Tofu Tête de Cochon* tastefully and decoratively. Leave room for the vegetables and add them when they're done.

REMOVE the Hell Turd remains and return with the *Tofu Tête de Cochon*. Blush slightly at the oohs and ahhs of your guests. Now you can sit down and, if you're still hungry, eat with your guests. Quietly relax with the knowledge you can make Robin do the dishes.

REMOVE the dinner plates but wait a while for dessert, since there are 50 more people arriving for that.

So now you know the process involved in throwing a lavish dinner party such as this one. Mostly it is a matter of planning and thinking ahead. Try not to forget that the whole point of the exercise is to have fun.

FUN WITH FOOD COLOURING

In his youth, Link Leisure, pop star, once served an all-black dinner (but he said to be sure to tell you he was never into Goth). There was black Kraft Dinner, black bread, and black butter, with black cheesecake for dessert. How did he perform this amazing feat? Why, through the miracle of food colouring.

Although it exists, black food colouring can be quite difficult to find, so here's an idea for those with limited free time: whip food colouring into cream cheese and serve it on celery sticks or crudités. For a more sophisticated application, place the cream cheese in a plastic bag and snip off a corner to make a piping bag.

WELL, I HAVE TO HAND IT TO ROBIN, SHE SORT OF PULLED THIS ONE OFF. HA HA! WHAT AN IMAGINATION! THE ALL CELEBRITY PARTY IS TOMORROW.

Did I forget anything?

SNIFF

WHAT IF NO ONE LIKES THE PARTY?

Let's see...Soup... check! Got my kit...Hell turds...check!

ACHOO!

...I feel awful... Cucumbers... check!

WHAT WILL I SAY TO JONI?

Robin said she would get some of that delicious coffee....... ...Tofu Tete de Cochon... check!

HONK

DID I FORGET ANYTHING?

#?@!

THE Cake!

THe Cake!

Basic Chocolate Cake

We make this when we can't get laid.

2 cups flour

1/2 cup plus 3 tbsp. cocoa

1 1/2 cups granulated white sugar

2 tsp. baking powder

1/2 tsp. baking soda

2 pinches of salt

1/2 cup cooking oil

1/2 cup strong coffee (or substitute water)

2/3 cup milk

2 eggs, beaten

1 tsp. pure vanilla extract

PREHEAT THE OVEN to 350°.

In a large bowl, sift together the flour, sugar, cocoa, salt, baking soda, and baking powder. Make a well in these ingredients, and put into it the oil, coffee, milk, eggs, and vanilla extract.

With an electric mixer on low speed, blend until all the ingredients are moistened. Mix a little longer at medium speed to ensure the batter is airy. Remember: an airy batter is a better batter.

Divide the mixture into two greased and floured 9-inch round cake pans and bake for 25-30 minutes, or until a toothpick poked into the centre emerges clean. Let cool before removing from pans.

Makes 2 9-inch cakes.

Butter Icing

"I can't wait to put the icing on the cake."—The B-52's

1/4 cup butter, at room temperature

3 1/2 cups sifted icing sugar

2 pinches salt

3 tbsp. whipping cream, or half and half, or milk

1 tsp. pure vanilla extract

food colouring to suit (if desired)

IN A LARGE BOWL, whip the butter with an electric mixer, then sift the salt and some of the sugar into the butter. Add it slowly with the mixer on low speed, unless you want sugar all over the walls, the floor, various counter surfaces, and you. When the mix gets too thick, add some of the wet ingredients, then more of the sugar. In this way you can control the viscosity of the final product. Icing doesn't have to be cooked, so you are free to play around with the proportions of ingredients to suit yourself. More butter produces a less sweet, smoother, and richer icing. For chocolate icing, add cocoa 'til it's chocolatey enough for you.

Makes enough for a 2-layer cake.

SMARTIE PARTY

Here's an elegant presentation idea for those who like to serve Smarties at their parties. Buy a large econo-pak of Smarties and pour them onto a baking sheet. Sort them according to colour and then serve them in a set of matching bowls. Reserve the red ones until after the others are consumed.

Variations:

Aunt Agnes' 12 Layer Cake

From the Queen of Cakes.

6 Basic Chocolate Cake recipes, pg. 64 (to make 12 round cakes)
6 Butter Icing recipes, pg. 65

FOLLOW THE INSTRUCTIONS as illustrated on page 68.

Loss of Job Cake

The beauty of this cake is that you must eat the whole thing in one sitting, due to its ice cream centre.

1 Basic Chocolate Cake, pg. 64

3 deluxe ice cream bars

1 pint whipping cream, whipped

1 pint fresh strawberries

WHEN YOUR CAKES have cooled, remove the sticks from the ice cream bars and place the bars on the first layer. Place the second layer on top.

Cover the sides and top with whipped cream, then on top of the cake spell with your finger the job title/name of ex-employer/field of employment, etc., followed by profanity.

Garnish the side of the cake with strawberries.

Eat with relish.

Variations:

Exploding Jesus Cake

Try multiplying this one, baby.

1 Basic Chocolate Cake, pg. 64, baked in a 9" x 12" pan

1 Butter Icing recipe, pg. 65

variety of fresh seasonal fruit, washed and peeled

1 small explosive device

4 cloves

AFTER THE CAKE is cooled, cut and arrange it as illustrated here:

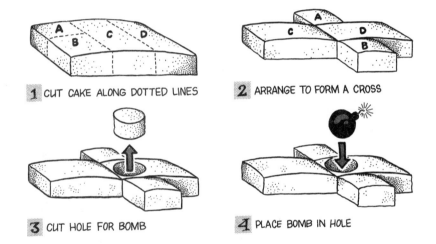

1 CUT CAKE ALONG DOTTED LINES

2 ARRANGE TO FORM A CROSS

3 CUT HOLE FOR BOMB

4 PLACE BOMB IN HOLE

Ice the cake, then form an image of Jesus Christ using chunks and slices of fruit on top of the cake. Use the cloves as nails on the hands and feet.

Explode when serving.

AROMATHERAPY SUCKS

Once Pierre and his niece, Allison, both jobless, were on Vancouver Island staying at his sister Beth's cottage on the beach. Since it was the rainy season they had no desire to go exploring. Usually Allison would take out her collection of shells and pebbles and obsessively line them up on the coffee table according to order of preference, and sometimes she and Pierre would sit around and think up atrocious and degrading things to call each other, but soon these activities grew thin and there was nothing left to do. They had already been barred from the Pig and Whistle Pub for unsavoury behaviour. Now they had a bad case of cabin fever.

They woke up one afternoon, and after bottomless pots of coffee and a "wake and bake" they were restless and irritable.

"Why are we staying here?" asked Pierre.

"So we don't have to look for a job," Allison replied. Reminded of this convenience, Pierre's spirits brightened for a moment, but then almost instantly returned to their now-familiar state of bored stupor.

cont'd

AUNT AGNES' 12 LAYER CAKE

1: BAKE 12 BASIC CHOCOLATE CAKES, ALL THE SAME SIZE

2: MAKE BUTTER ICING WHILE THE CAKES COOL

HOMO MILK

BUTTER

SUGAR

HAVE YOU SEEN THIS CHILD?

3: ICE EACH CAKE INDI-VIDUALLY AND LAYER

IF THE CAKES ARE TOO ROUND SLICE OFF THE TOPS...

...AND MAKE **RUMBALLS**

MISC.

← RUM

NUTS ↗

CAKE BITS

SQUISH IT ALL TOGETHER

4: EAT **RUMBALLS**

HIC

5: DECORATE CAKE WITH ANYTHING HANDY

SOME SUGGESTIONS:

RARE

DON'T USE THINGS THAT LOOK LIKE FOOD BUT AREN'T FOOD

¡VOILA!

6: SIT BACK AND AWAIT LAVISH COMPLIMENTS **SERVES FIFTY!**

"Hey, what's left in the cupboard?" said Allison, changing the subject.

"Well, we drank all the booze, so there's just that cake mix left," Pierre replied. "Wanna bake a cake?"

They were interrupted by the ring of the phone, which Allison answered to discover her sister Jennifer on the line. Jennifer was distraught. She had been late for work at the aromatherapy boutique and her new age hippie boss had given her the boot. She was calling from a pay phone on the ferry, and was coming to join the ranks of the unemployed.

Suddenly inspired by consolatory feelings for Jennifer, the niece and uncle determined to bake her the cake. Within the next hour they dirtied every utensil in the kitchen as they sang, "If I knew you were coming I'd have baked a cake," and, from this, the very first Loss of Job Cake was born. Clumsily covered with whipped cream, it looked hideous and naïve.

"Shall we write something on it?" suggested Pierre.

Allison momentarily pondered. "How about `AROMATHERAPY SUCKS'?"

Allison used her finger to carefully spell out the words on the cake and then they decorated it a bit more with strawberries around the edge. They looked at it with the pride of achievement and hatred of employer intolerance.

"F#$king capitalist hippie," muttered Pierre.

"Bloody patriarch," supplied Allison.

Soon after Jen arrived, and, when she was presented with the cake, she got even more upset and began to cry.

"You're mocking me!" she tearfully accused.

Pierre and Allison were devastated. All this work, only to have Jennifer refuse the gift. Sometimes life just goes that way. "You really pick my ass," Pierre said, exasperated. "I'm ready to go back to the city."

And he did, on the very next ferry.

WHEN THE NEIGHBOURS COMPLAIN

If a police officer comes to your door, don't offer him a toke.

Rumballs

Don't eat these and drive.

1/4 cup butter, at room temperature

1 1/2 cups icing sugar

1 cup cocoa

4 cups dried-out cake crumbs

3/4 cup dark rum

1 cup roasted almonds, chopped

1/2 cup raisins (optional)

8 ounces fine quality chocolate

IN A LARGE BOWL, beat the butter with an electric mixer at low speed. Add 1/2 cup icing sugar and integrate well. Take the rest of the icing sugar, cocoa, cake crumbs, and rum and add about 1/2 cup each at a time, except the rum, which should be added 1/4 cup at a time. The idea is to rotate the wet and dry ingredients so as not to over-strain your mixer. Keep going until it's all in the mix. Then add the nuts and optional raisins and mix them in with your hands.

Roll into balls and refrigerate.

In a double boiler over low heat, melt the chocolate, stirring occasionally. When it has a liquid consistency, dip each ball individually into the chocolate to completely cover it. You can then also roll the chocolate-covered rumballs in chocolate vermicelli, roasted nuts, or icing sugar if you want to.

Place onto a cookie sheet and refrigerate. Rumballs should not be consumed until at least 12 hours after their creation in order to let the rum flavour cure.

Makes 40 rumballs.

STOCKING THE LIQUOR CABINET

Have a BYOB party and invite at least 20 people. After they have all arrived and stored their booze in the fridge, pretend to get a phone call from the hospital. Tell your guests it's a family emergency and that they all must leave. Act as if you're so distraught you don't think of giving them their booze back before they go. (For extra effective faux distress, sniff a freshly chopped onion or pluck out a nose hair while on the phone.) If your guests are like ours, they'll fall for it every time.

Crustini

Sort of like a cracker but better.

1 baguette cut into 1/4 inch slices
3 cloves garlic, skinned but whole
about 1/4 cup olive oil

PREHEAT THE OVEN to 350°.

Place the slices of bread onto a baking sheet and place in the oven for 3 to 5 minutes to dry them out and get them ready for crustininess. Remove the tray from the oven and lightly drizzle olive oil onto each bread piece. Return them to the oven for another 5-8 minutes, or until the pieces are golden brown.

Remove them from the oven again and let them cool slightly. Lull yourself into a trance-like state, then rub them individually with the whole cloves of garlic. The coarse texture of the bread will have a slight grater-like effect on the garlic. Crustinis are great instead of melba toast in the making of *hors d'oeuvres.*

Makes about 50 slices.

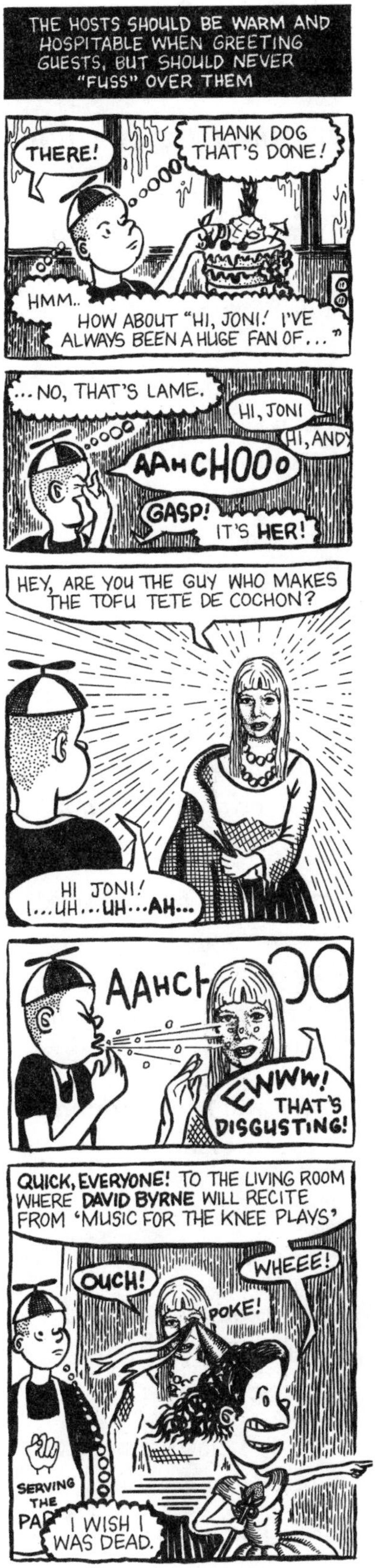
THE HOSTS SHOULD BE WARM AND HOSPITABLE WHEN GREETING GUESTS, BUT SHOULD NEVER "FUSS" OVER THEM
THERE!
THANK DOG THAT'S DONE!
HMM.. HOW ABOUT "HI, JONI! I'VE ALWAYS BEEN A HUGE FAN OF..."
...NO, THAT'S LAME.
HI, JONI
HI, ANDY
AAHCHOOO
GASP! IT'S HER!
HEY, ARE YOU THE GUY WHO MAKES THE TOFU TETE DE COCHON?
HI JONI! I...UH...UH...AH...
AAHCHOO
EWWW! THAT'S DISGUSTING!
QUICK, EVERYONE! TO THE LIVING ROOM WHERE DAVID BYRNE WILL RECITE FROM 'MUSIC FOR THE KNEE PLAYS'
OUCH!
WHEEE!
POKE!
SERVING THE PA
I WISH I WAS DEAD.

PERSONALIZED FORTUNE COOKIES

This is fun and easy to do. Go to Chinatown and buy some fortune cookies. Later at home, use a pair of tweezers to carefully remove the fortunes from inside the cookies. Usually the cookies aren't completely closed and there is a bit of a slit you can fit the tweezers through if you're careful; but if it is closed you may have a make a little hole (or just eat it— problem solved!). Gather up those fortunes and throw them away.

Now cut out fortune-sized pieces of paper and write your own fortunes on them. We try to write things that we know are true, such as:

> You will have a fortune cookie today.

or

> Someday you will die.

Or you can write things that are advantageous to yourself, such as:

> Giving Pierre money will bring you great luck.

> Kissing Robin will bring serenity.

cont'd

THE ENDLESS JAM

One night Pierre went all the way to Amsterdam for a dinner at Omar's fab pad by the canal, where he was pleased to find his old friend, Jopie, who was always a source of surprise and entertainment. As Omar bounded around in the kitchen, Pierre and Jopie sat in the garden and caught up on things. Enjoying the novelty of being blatant, Pierre rolled a predinner joint out there and lit it. He offered it to Jopie who accepted without hesitation, and took two mega hits. This was not noted as anything out of the ordinary by Pierre, who had the popular misconception that all Amsterdamsters are constantly stoned. Jopie passed the joint back, then commenced a long and tedious monologue that didn't make much sense, sometimes substituting random sounds for words. On the next round of tokes Pierre considerately thought to remove the joint to the kitchen so Omar could also partake of it.

In the kitchen they found Omar toasting some large round cracker-like things directly over the gas element of his stove.

Jopie was amazed. "What is that?" he asked.

"It's poppadum," replied Omar.

Immediately Jopie picked up a knife and fork and began to beat a tempo on the various dishware cluttering the counters. He commenced to sing, in his jazzy way, "poppadum, poppadum-dum!"

Pierre was amused at first, but Omar quickly realized what was going on.

"Oh, no," he lamented. "Did Jopie smoke this joint?"

"Well, yeah," yelled Pierre over Jopie's din. "So?"

"Have you ever seen Jopie stoned before?"

After thinking for a second or two Pierre realized he never had.

"Well, now you're gonna get it."

Pierre and Omar ate dinner. Jopie did not, for he was consumed by the rhythmical trance of "poppadum, poppadum-dum, poppadum, poppadum-dum, poppadum." This went on for hours until Jopie passed out on the couch. Pierre and Omar were very annoyed and said bad things about Jopie and never offered to get him stoned again.

Poppadums

This wins the prize for Scrambled Brains' *easiest recipe.*

GO TO LITTLE INDIA and buy Poppadums—large Indian crackers that usually come in a little box or a bag with "Poppadum" or "Pappadam" written on it. Reasonably priced, they are made mainly with lentil flour, and are available in a variety of flavours, such as Cayenne, Garlic, Caraway Seed, Cracked Black Pepper, and many many more, and are always a sure-fire hit.

At home, turn on an element on your stove top, and with a pair of tongs place one Poppadum onto the bare element. Flip the Poppadum constantly with the tongs. It will start to bubble and become lighter in weight and colour as it cooks, then it will become crispy with little black spots. This process happens over a very short time, about 15 seconds. Set the cooked Poppadum aside and start a new one, and repeat until you have the desired amount.

(This one's risky—you never know who will get it.)

Obviously what is true and advantageous will change according to circumstances. Take your written fortunes and slide them into the cookies. Tell your guests you make the cookies from scratch, but you can't give out the recipe because it's a family secret that's been passed down through generations.

YOU ARE LOOKING AT A COOKBOOK

DIP TIPS

All the dips and crackers in this chapter can be used on their own, or mixed and matched. For a swanky hors d'oeuvre try spreading tapenade on crustini, then top with marinated bell pepper. Pay attention to detail: May we suggest a chiffonade of fresh basil as a garnish?

HOW TO PICK YOUR PEPPERS

Select peppers that are a squarish shape and try to cut them so that the quarters will lay as flat as possible. The goal here is maximum contact between the skin of the peppers and the bottom of the pan.

These will get your tastebuds ringing.

4 red bell peppers, quartered and seeded

2 tbsp. freshly chopped basil

2 tbsp. balsamic or red wine vinegar (sherry is also good)

2 tbsp. olive oil

salt and pepper to taste

HEAT A CAST-IRON SKILLET over high heat. Rub the pepper pieces with a little bit of the oil and a pinch of salt, and set the peppers skin side down into the smoking pan. Cover with a lid. Cook at high heat until the skin is charred and the flesh is tender, about 10 minutes.

When the peppers are ready, place them in a sealed, air-tight container. This process is called "sweating." It permits the peppers to finish cooking. Let them sweat for 30 minutes. By this point the charred skin should come off very easily by scraping it with a knife. We have heard that burnt food is very carcinogenic, so please be thorough. Strain the juices of the pepper and reserve for marinade.

Slice the peppers lengthwise, julienne style. Combine the vinegar, basil, salt, pepper, strained juices, and remaining olive oil and place the sliced bell peppers in it, and let sit for at least an hour before serving.

Makes about a cup.

Tapenade

Don't let its colour put you off.

1 tin pitted black olives, drained, rinsed, and coarsely chopped

1/2 white onion, diced

3 cloves garlic, crushed

1/4 cup olive oil

2 tsp. fresh rosemary, finely chopped

2 tbsp. fresh parsley, chopped

1 tbsp. tomato paste

3 anchovy fillets, patted dry and coarsely chopped (optional)

splash of red wine (optional)

juice of 1 lemon

salt and pepper to taste

HEAT A DRY cast-iron skillet over high heat. Add the tomato paste to the hot pan with a wooden spoon, and scrape and smear the paste around until it has rendered most of its humidity and starts to turn brown. This is called "browning the paste." Pour in half of the oil and quickly add the onions and garlic. Keep scraping the paste from the bottom of the pan and mix it in thoroughly.

Add the remaining ingredients into the pan and continue cooking over a medium high heat for 5 minutes, stirring occasionally. Season to taste.

Remove the mixture from the heat and then put it into a food processor*. Process it fairly coarse so that the ingredients are still distinguishable.

Place the tapenade into a bowl and let cool. Pour the remaining oil over top. It is best to refrigerate this overnight and then serve it at room temperature with bread or crustini (pg. 71).

Makes about 2 cups.

*A blender will not work for this recipe. You must use a food processor or chop it by hand.

TOMATO PASTE

Browning the tomato paste as described in this recipe is a good way of removing its acidity. You can also flavour the paste with herbs and seasonings, and you can do a whole tin at once if you want to. To store paste not for immediate use, place it in an airtight container and pour in enough olive oil to cover its entire surface. This will prevent air from getting into it. It will keep in your refrigerator for about a month.

L'Anchoyade

A dip for blanched vegetables or a spread for crackers. Not usually made with mayonnaise, but we like it this way.

1 cup mayonnaise, pg. 18

juice of 2 lemons

3 cloves garlic, finely minced

4 anchovy fillets, patted dry and finely chopped

fresh ground pepper to taste

COMBINE all ingredients.

Makes 1 cup.

L'ANCHOYADE a la KATHY O

THE NAKED DINNER PARTY

BUDGET: Being bored living in the city where nothing ever happens, Pierre and Robin, along with some friends, produced a one-night-only, smash hit stage production entitled "A Blood Red Cabaret." With the $44 they made, they decided to host a thank-you party for all the participants: a Naked Dinner Party.

INVITATIONS: Co-host and cabaret star Flopper Al made a skillfully assembled photomontage depicting a naked lady salad.

DECOR: Creative energy perpetuates itself, so Al then turned his efforts to decor. Deciding to go for an Adam and Eve look, he proceeded to raid the neighbourhood for bags and bags of vines to hang in the windows. Ever zealous, he collected a deluxe amount and soon transformed the apartment with cascades of purloined ivy, giving it the atmosphere of a garden or jungle.

ATTIRE: Since it was a Naked Dinner Party, no attire was allowed.

GUESTS: Surprisingly, many people balk at the idea of eating in their birthday suits, so to speak, so the guests who attended were adventurous, free-thinking radicals, or perhaps just perves. At any rate it was a stimulating mix of happy, naked people wearing their favourite accessories.

MENU: Flopper Al insisted on a buffet consisting of 5-bean salad and Kraft Dinner with tofu wieners. Pierre, with his more upper crust palate, salved his disturbed culinary sensibilities by preparing and presenting *L'Anchoyade à la Kathy O* as an appetizer.

PRESENTATION: Kathy's reclined naked body was covered artistically with steamed romaine lettuce leaves, and she sported Swiss cheese slices and radishes on her nipples. Between her legs was a hollow half red pepper filled with *L'Anchoyade*, the popular anchovy mayonnaise sauce, and she held a baguette in her hands for dipping.

APRÈS DINNER ACTIVITIES: Pot was smoked, a snake was fondled, frenzied naked lip-synching was performed, and one of the guests got a hard-on.

a Short Seminar on Blanched Vegetables

ZIPPY BLANCH

(3 minutes or less)

Green onions
Snow peas
Broccoli
Spinach
Zucchini

MIDDLE BLANCH

(3 to 5 minutes)

Bell peppers
Green beans
Asparagus
Corn
Mushrooms
Leeks
Squash

EXTENDO BLANCH

(5 to 8 minutes)

Carrots
Celery
Celeriac
Rutabagas
Parsnip
Cauliflower

Some vegetables, such as raw beet root, potatoes, artichoke hearts, and Jerusalem artichokes, don't blanch very well. They need to be either steamed or boiled.

OUR FAVOURITE way to have *L'Anchoyade* is with chilled blanched vegetables. It's a bit more fuss than serving *crudités**, but worth it for those with a craving for the uncommon. When preparing this dish, we select a variety of at least 7 vegetables. You can plan 1 piece of each vegetable per person eating, unless of course, some of your guests are gluttons. But usually the anorexic types will even the balance.

Place a large pot of water to boil.

Prepare the vegetables by washing, peeling, and slicing them into attractive dipping-sized pieces (see note). Blanch the vegetable types individually, as they have different cooking times (see the sidebar).

To halt the cooking process, you must douse the vegetables in ice cold water, and leave them until they have completely chilled. This process will seal in their nutrients and maintain their bright colours. In a pinch you can blanch the vegetables the day before they will be served, but in most instances it is best to do it on the same day. Serve chilled.

* raw vegetables

VEGETABLE SLICE SIZES: *This is what we call the "Lipstick Trick." Food chunks should be small enough so that Granny can eat them without smudging her lipstick. Pick up a chunk and put it in your mouth. If you cannot avoid touching your lips, your chunks are too large. As a rule of thumb, this can be applied to anything you are cutting into bite-sized pieces.*

* SOCIAL STUDIES BY DAVID BYRNE

Tabbouleh

This is a parsley salad with bulgur wheat, not a bulgur wheat salad with parsley.

2 firmly packed cups parsley, finely chopped

1/4 cup mint leaves, finely chopped

1/4 cup fine bulgur wheat, presoaked for an hour

1 onion, finely diced

1 large tomato, cut into cubes

1/3 cup lemon juice

1/4 cup extra virgin olive oil

salt and cayenne pepper to taste

CHOPPING UP all that parsley is more time consuming than you think, so do it while the bulgur wheat is presoaking. When you chop the parsley it will release some of its juices, so it is recommended that you blot it in a dishtowel before using it to ensure the salad does not turn out mushy. For more information on chopped parsley, see the following page.

Take the presoaked bulgur wheat and with your hands squeeze out any excess liquid. In a large mixing bowl, mix the ingredients together in order of appearance, with a motion that is a cross between a stir and a salad toss. Don't question your stirring adequacy if you can't quite accomplish this move at first. Such finesse even takes tabbouleh experts years to master. However, should you succeed, you will be rewarded with a lighter, fluffier salad.

No matter how you stir it, be sure to get the ingredients well mixed. Season to taste.

Serve chilled.

Makes 4-6 servings.

ALL ABOUT CHOPPED PARSLEY: After you've recovered from the trauma of chopping all that parsley, you must return to it and make sure it is indeed *finely* chopped. Parsley is a very coarse herb, so for salad-making purposes the finer it's chopped the more palatable it is.

Once Pierre worked with an eccentric old chef from Switzerland who asked him to chop some parsley. After washing and drying it, Pierre held a bunch by the stems, placed it on his cutting board, and shaved the leaves off by scraping them with the edge of his large chef's knife. Then he got out another large knife.

"I'll impress this eccentric chef with some old school ways," he thought as he lined up the parsley in a long rectangular pile on the cutting board. "It's showtime."

With a knife in each hand, held one inch apart, he proceeded to chop in a one-two tempo, occasionally scooping it back into its rectangular pattern before chopping more. He increased his rhythm as it became finer and finer. By now he had the attention of everyone in the kitchen, including the chef's.

He came to Pierre, yelling "*Mais, qu'est-ce que tu fais?* What are you doing?"

"I'm chopping parsley," Pierre replied.

"*Maudit!* We are in America, you know?" He grabbed the cutting board and dumped the parsley into the industrial food processor, spastically operating the pulse button while he mumbled obscene curses in French.

He showed Pierre his machine-chopped result.

"*Voilà,*" he said. "American parsley."

So it's up to you how the parsley gets chopped, but if the blades on your food processor are dull you will not get good results. We suggest a combination of both methods, doing the hand chopping last to make sure the parsley has a consistent texture.

Roasted Oyster Mushroom and Bocconcini Salad

Especially enjoyable atop fresh dandelion greens.

1 pound oyster mushrooms (or less, if you're stingy)

2 tbsp. butter

3 cloves garlic

1 tsp. fresh sage, finely chopped

1 tbsp. fresh parsley, finely chopped

4 balls of bocconcini

2 tbsp. olive oil

salt and pepper to taste

1 pound, more or less, of salad greens of your choice

4-5 ounces vinaigrette (see pg. 111)

HEAT A SKILLET over medium low heat and add the butter, garlic, and parsley. Let sit for a few minutes, stirring occasionally, to let the garlic flavour infuse into the butter.

If the oyster mushrooms are in a cluster, break them apart into individual mushrooms, keeping the stems intact. Place the oyster mushrooms stem side up into the pan containing the garlic butter and, still over medium low heat, cook for 5 minutes or until the mushrooms are soft and tender. Season to taste, remove from heat, and let cool.

Preheat the oven to 400°.

On a greased baking sheet, portion the mushrooms into decorative clusters with the tops facing up and the stems pointing in. Make one cluster for each person eating. Cut each bocconcini into 4 round slices, then arrange the slices in the centres of the mushroom clusters. Sprinkle each cluster with sage and parsley, then olive oil. Season to taste.

Roast in the oven for about 5-10 minutes, or until the cheese is thoroughly warmed and begins to melt.

Put the greens on salad plates and top with one mushroom cluster each. Serve immediately, with vinaigrette on the side.

Makes 4 appetizer-sized salads.

A DANDELION IN SPRING

Jimmy B's Slaw

According to Jimmy B, this refreshing coleslaw is even better the next day, but it's so good it never makes it past the dinner table.

1 small green cabbage, shredded

1/2 red cabbage, shredded

3 carrots, grated

1 onion, finely diced

4 to 5 green onions, chopped

4 tbsp. white vinegar

1/2 cup raisins

1 big, firm apple, cut into small cubes

2 cups mayonnaise

juice of 2 lemons

salt and pepper to taste

POUR THE JUICE of 1 lemon into a large mixing bowl and swirl it around so that the juice coats the inside of the entire bowl. Refrigerate this while you chop the vegetables.

Once the bowl is chilled, add the cabbages, carrots, and onions, and mix thoroughly. Season to taste, then one at a time stir in the vinegar, raisins, apple cubes, the juice of the other lemon, and mayonnaise. Let chill and serve.

Makes 4-6 servings.

Hell Turds

Named for their hot flavour and bright red interior, just like H-E-double hockey sticks.

1 cup dried chickpeas, soaked overnight

2 tbsp. fresh ginger, coarsely chopped

4 cloves garlic, crushed

3 red hot chili peppers, seeded and quartered

1/2 cup coarsely chopped coriander, parsley, and celery leaf

3 whole green onions

4 tbsp. bulgur wheat

1/4 cup water

juice of 1 lemon

2 pinches of salt

pinch of garam masala (an Indian spice mixture)

1/4 cup sesame seeds, dry roasted

1/2 cup grated raw beet root

4 tbsp. or more oil for frying

IN THE FOOD PROCESSOR that you borrowed from your neighbour and failed to return, mix the ginger, garlic, chili peppers, herbs, and onions and grind into a paste. Gradually add the raw chickpeas, lemon juice, water, and bulgur wheat and grind until smooth. Place in a bowl and add the garam masala, sesame seeds, and beet root, and mix with your hands to make a pretty purple pasty mush. Form into small bite-sized patties.

Preheat a skillet over high heat and coat the bottom with a generous amount of oil. Make sure the oil is hot or the turds will stick.

Place the turds individually in the skillet and fry until all the turds are a beautiful dark browny red (about 4 minutes), then turn them over and cook them on the other side (about another 4 minutes). Once they are cooked, place them on a paper towel or clean dry cloth to soak up the excess fat.

PARTY!

You can serve Hell Turds any way you want, but we like to serve them with Lemon Yoghurt and Salted Cucumbers. They are neutral condiments that soothe the palate.

For individual and beautifully presented portions, place 3 or 4 Hell Turds in a semi-circle on a fancy plate. Beside them spoon out some Lemon Yoghurt and place a large tablespoonful of cucumber slices on top of the yoghurt. Garnish with a fresh mint leaf.

Makes 36 turds.

1 cucumber, peeled, halved, seeded, and sliced paper thin at an exact 45° angle

1 tsp. salt, or to taste

Mix together and let sit in a strainer for at least half an hour. This will allow the salt to bring out the juices of the cucumber.

LEMON YOGHURT

1/2 cup yoghurt

juice of 1 lemon

Mix together.

ROASTED OYSTER MUSHROOM AND BOCCONCINI SALAD

I WISH IT WAS A COOKIE

THE HOST SHOULD REMAIN PLEASANT UNDER ANY CIRCUMSTANCES. ANYTHING ELSE IS BAD MANNERS AND A **SIN** AGAINST ETIQUETTE

DingDong

I'LL GET IT!

I CAN'T EAT THIS. I **TOLD** YOU, I'M LACTOSE INTOLERANT.

PERHAPS IT'S WILLIAM S. BURROUGHS, ARRIVING LATE...

HELLO?

HI! I'M **JESUS CHRIST**, AND I'M HERE FOR 'THE **FREE** TOFU TETE DE COCHON

YOU'RE **NOT** JESUS CHRIST

YOU'RE THE **LATE** JERRY GARCIA OF THE GRATEFUL DEAD!

GET LOST!

YOU **WEREN'T** INVITED HERE

GO AWAY YOU HYPOCRITICAL CAPITALIST HIPPIE!

BUT I—

YOU **MAKE** ME SICK!

GO ON! GET OUT OF HERE, YOU— YOU **CROUTON!**

ALRIGHT, ALRIGHT...

GEEZ

'CROUTON'?

NOT TO BE CONFUSED WITH 'CRETIN', WHICH ARE FOUND IN SUCH ABUNDANCE IN NORTH AMERICA THERE'S NO NEED TO MAKE YOUR OWN

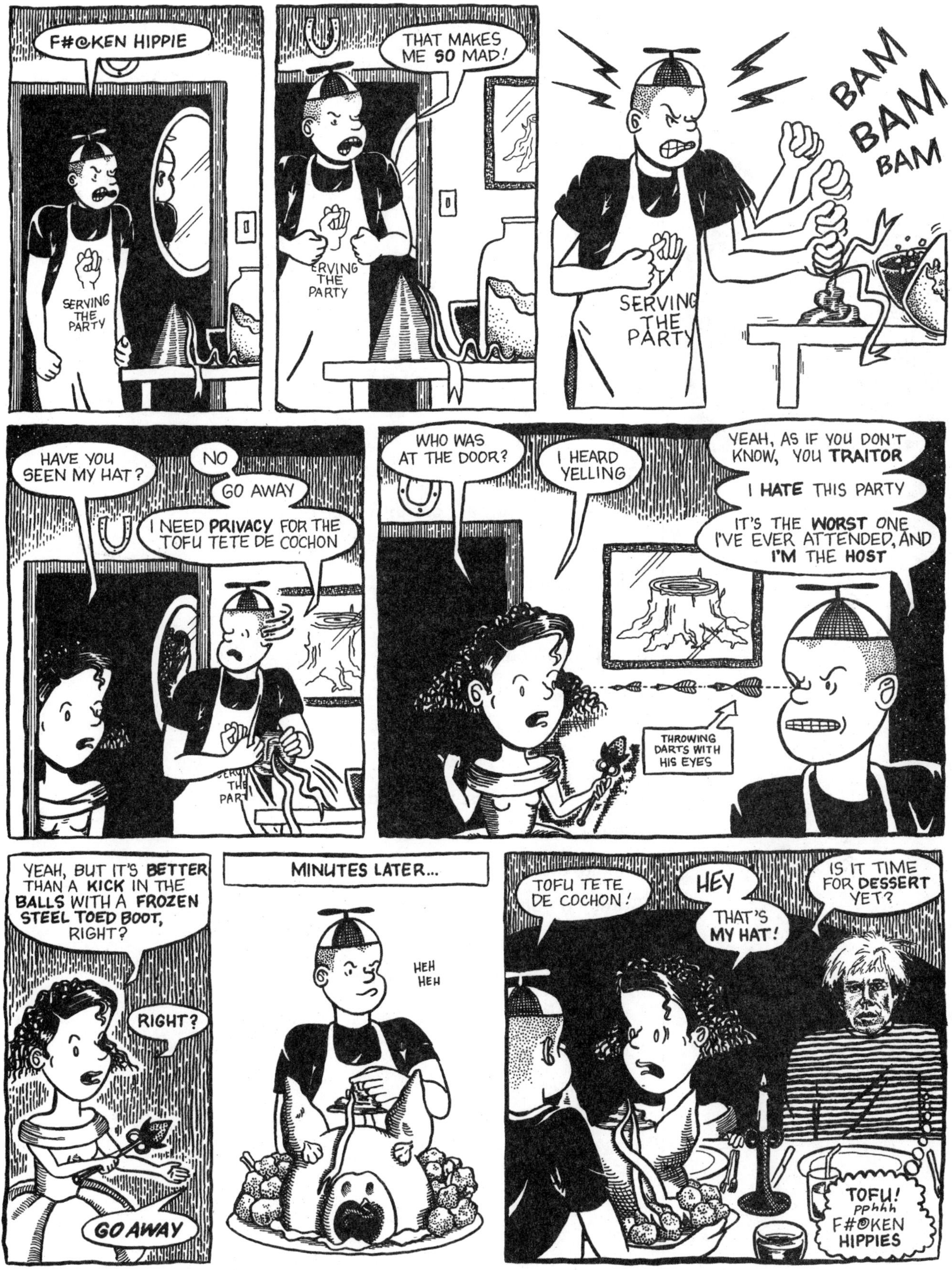
F#@KEN HIPPIE
SERVING THE PARTY
THAT MAKES ME SO MAD!
SERVING THE PARTY
SERVING THE PARTY
BAM BAM BAM
HAVE YOU SEEN MY HAT?
NO
GO AWAY
I NEED PRIVACY FOR THE TOFU TETE DE COCHON
WHO WAS AT THE DOOR?
I HEARD YELLING
YEAH, AS IF YOU DON'T KNOW, YOU TRAITOR
I HATE THIS PARTY
IT'S THE WORST ONE I'VE EVER ATTENDED, AND I'M THE HOST
THROWING DARTS WITH HIS EYES
YEAH, BUT IT'S BETTER THAN A KICK IN THE BALLS WITH A FROZEN STEEL TOED BOOT, RIGHT?
RIGHT?
GO AWAY
MINUTES LATER...
HEH HEH
TOFU TETE DE COCHON!
HEY
THAT'S MY HAT!
IS IT TIME FOR DESSERT YET?
TOFU! pphhh F#@KEN HIPPIES

Tofu Tête de Cochon

Don't let the long list of ingredients scare you: the preparation of this recipe is a party in itself.

TOFU MIXTURE:

4 pounds firm tofu

2 tbsp. soy sauce

1 tbsp. Dijon mustard

1 tsp. Chinese 5-spice powder

STUFFING:

6 slices hearty bread, cut into cubes

1 onion, diced

2 stalks celery, finely chopped

1/2 red bell pepper, diced

3 tbsp. olive oil

1/2 cup water or vegetable broth

1 tbsp. soy sauce (optional)

2 carrots grated

1 cup pecans, coarsely ground

1/2 cup raisins

1 apple, diced

3 green onions, chopped

1/2 cup parsley, finely chopped

1/4 cup celery leaves, chiffonade

1 tsp. fresh thyme

1 tbsp. zest of orange

juice of one orange

salt and pepper to taste

BASTING MIXTURE:

1/4 cup oil

2 cloves garlic, finely minced

2 tbsp. kecap manis (sweet soy sauce)

1 tbsp. paprika (for colour)

pinch of Chinese 5-spice powder

GARNISH:

1 apple

2 whole bulbs of garlic, unpeeled

WITH YOUR TRUSTY food processor, add all of the tofu mixture ingredients. Push the "on" button and wait patiently until it has transformed into a silky paste. Pour the mix into another container and refrigerate a little bit, but not enough to make it firm again.

For the stuffing, place a large, thick-bottomed pot over medium heat, and pour in the olive oil. When it's hot, sauté the onions, celery, and bell peppers with a pinch of salt for 3 minutes. Gradually add the bread cubes and gently toss with 2 wooden spoons until the bread is thoroughly assimilated into the mixture. You have to be attentive here because you don't want the bread to get mushy. What you seek is the perfect balance of coated yet firm. Add the water (or broth) and soy sauce and gently toss for another 3 minutes. Remove from heat and add the remaining stuffing ingredients, tossing between each one. Season to taste.

Here comes the fun part. Now, we don't know anyone who owns a pig's head-shaped mold, but it would make life easier. If you have one, goody for you. If you don't, like most of us, your creative powers will need to come into play. Start with the main form of the head. For ease, use a large bowl. It's important that the diameter of the bowl does not exceed the width of your baking sheet. Line the inside of the bowl with plastic wrap, leaving the edges of the wrap on the outside of the bowl. Get your tofu mixture and set aside 1/3

EXPERIMENTS IN TOFU

This recipe makes the head of a pig, but the brighter among you have realized you can make most anything you can imagine. We at the Scrambled Brains Laboratory tried many, many forms before we came up with the perfect one. Our experiments have included:

Fish
Turtle
Pumpkin
Mud puddle
Mount Rushmore
Stonehenge
Chicken
Moose
Doughnut
Ouija Board
Fire truck
Venus of Willendorf

We haven't tried every possible shape, but so far none of them have worked as well as the head of a pig.

TOFU CHICKEN

of it for the snout.

Your goal now is to line the inside of the bowl with the tofu, 1/2-inch to 3/4-inch thick. The easiest way we've discovered is to plop the tofu in in increments and spread it around with a spatula until you have a uniformly tofu-lined bowl. It is not necessary to go to the very rim of the bowl; 3/4 of the way up will do. You still have tofu left, don't you? Well, don't worry, you're going to use it all.

Take about 3/4 of the stuffing and fill the tofu-lined bowl. You have to do it in increments, tamping it down gently in between each one. Don't try to make it all fit if it doesn't. Just fill it up to 1/2-inch below the edge of the tofu lining. Now take some more tofu and spread it across the top, about 1/2-inch thick. Spread it around with a spatula to make it smooth and even.

To make the snout you basically repeat the process using a snout-shaped container, such as a small coffee can, yoghurt container, or whatever you think will work. But don't line the top with tofu.

For this recipe to work you must refrigerate both these elements for a while, at least 20 minutes, to allow the tofu to firm up enough that it will retain its shape.

Preheat the oven to 400°.

Take the bowl from the fridge and place the baking sheet on top, then turn the whole thing over. Try to get it on one end of the sheet rather than in the middle, as you need room for the snout. Remove the bowl. (The plastic lining edge is your friend for this manoeuvre.) Remove the plastic lining. You now have a stuffed tofu head.

Unmold the snout and place it on the tofu head. It's actually not so easy, for the tofu is firm enough by now that it will crack if you try to adjust its shape. However, you should still have some of the tofu mixture left, so use it to hide seams or fill in any boo-boos you might make. Cut a hole out of the end of the snout and stick the apple in it, so it protrudes about halfway out.

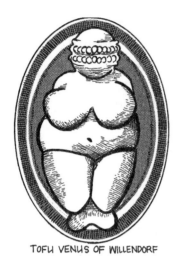

TOFU VENUS OF WILLENDORF

Take the 2 whole bulbs of garlic and try to cut out that woody bit in the middle. You know the one we mean? It's that part where all the cloves come together. In the recess that's left, pour a bit of olive oil, as much as it will retain.

Back to the pig's head. Cut garlic bulb-sized holes out of the tofu lining where you want the eyes to be and set the garlic bulbs in them, oil-filled recess sides down.

Mix the basting ingredients together and brush it all over the tofu pig's head. Bake for about 50 minutes, or until the apple is completely cooked. Baste it again once or twice while its baking.

This head has no ears yet, so when it's done make some from paper and stick them on. This is the easiest way, but you could also cut them out of firm tofu and put them on before the baking, or even make ears stuffed with filling (if you don't have a life).

You can't really remove the head from the baking sheet without destroying it (at least we never could), so may we suggest you place the baking sheet on a large cutting board or something similar, and disguise the sheet with lettuce, garnish, and steamed vegetables.

We have to admit this doesn't look exactly like Robin's amazing depictions, but this dish is still an eye-popper. Don't worry about leftovers. If you have any, see the wonderful veggie burger recipe sidebar. It's a leftover *Tofu Tête de Cochon* breakthrough!

Serves 10 vegetarians, or 16 meat eaters.

LEFTOVER *TOFU TÊTE DE COCHON* VEGGIE BURGERS

1 1/4 cups milled grain cereal

1 cup puréed leftover *Tofu Tête de Cochon*

2 cloves garlic, minced

1 tbsp. soy sauce

1 tsp. hot sauce

1 1/2 tsp. cumin

salt and pepper to taste

MIX ALL the ingredients together. Form into hamburger-like patties.

Cook in a greased skillet over medium heat until both sides are golden brown. Season to taste. Serve with buns and condiments of your choice. Try it with some aioli, pg. 19.

Makes 4 patties.

THE DEVIL Made Me Do It!

eggs

THIS PRESENTATION IDEA PREMIÈRED AT ROBIN'S ART SHOW 'THE DEVIL **MADE** ME DO IT' TO CREATE THIS FANCY SNACK YOU **MUST** MAKE THIS STENCIL:

ON A THIN PIECE OF PAPER DRAW A PITCHFORK ABOUT THIS SIZE:

TAPE THE PAPER DRAWING SIDE DOWN ONTO A SMALL PIECE OF SEE THROUGH MYLAR OR THIN SEMI-RIGID PLASTIC. FLIP IT OVER.

NOW, WITH A SHARP X-ACTO OR UTILITY KNIFE CAREFULLY CUT OUT YOUR SHAPE. NOTE THAT YOU CAN CUT THE POSITIVE IMAGE TO SHREDS BUT AVOID CUTS INTO THE NEGATIVE. REMOVE THE PAPER AND TAPE.

■ POSITIVE
▦ NEGATIVE

SCORE* THE MYLAR IN A SLIGHT CURVE AS ILLUSTRATED. IT'S A LITTLE TRICKY SO TRY VISUALIZING ½ AN EGG WHILE YOU DO IT. IT DOESN'T HAVE TO BE PERFECT.

SCORE THIS

VISUALIZE THIS

CUT INTO BOTH ENDS OF THE SCORED LINE A BIT. LIKE THIS:

CUT THE SOLID BLACK LINE

FLIP IT OVER AND BEND UP THE FLAP.

YOLK GUARD

READY for ACTION!

*SCORE: MAKE AN INCISION <u>ON</u> BUT NOT THROUGH THE SURFACE OF THE MYLAR

The Devil Made Me Do It Eggs

A favourite at the bridge club.

12 eggs, hard boiled, peeled and halved

3 tbsp. mayonnaise, pg. 18

1/4 tsp. mustard powder

1 shallot, finely minced

48 bits of red bell pepper cut into little horn shapes

paprika powder for stencilling

salt and cayenne pepper to taste

TO START, cut out a stencil as illustrated opposite. Spoon out all the egg yolks and place them in a bowl. Add mayonnaise, mustard powder, shallot, cayenne pepper, and salt. Mix vigorously until you have obtained an even texture. Spoon equal amounts of this filling into the egg hole where the yolk used to be. Stick the bell pepper pieces into the sides of the filling to simulate the Devil's "look."

Place the stencil onto the egg, sprinkle some paprika on the stencil, and gently push it into the cut-out areas with your finger. If you put too much on it will bleed around the edges and blur the Devil's pitchfork. If you don't put enough, the image will be obscure and undefined. Don't be shy, though, because if you make a mistake you can just carefully wipe it off and start over. Fun for the whole family!

Makes 24 servings.

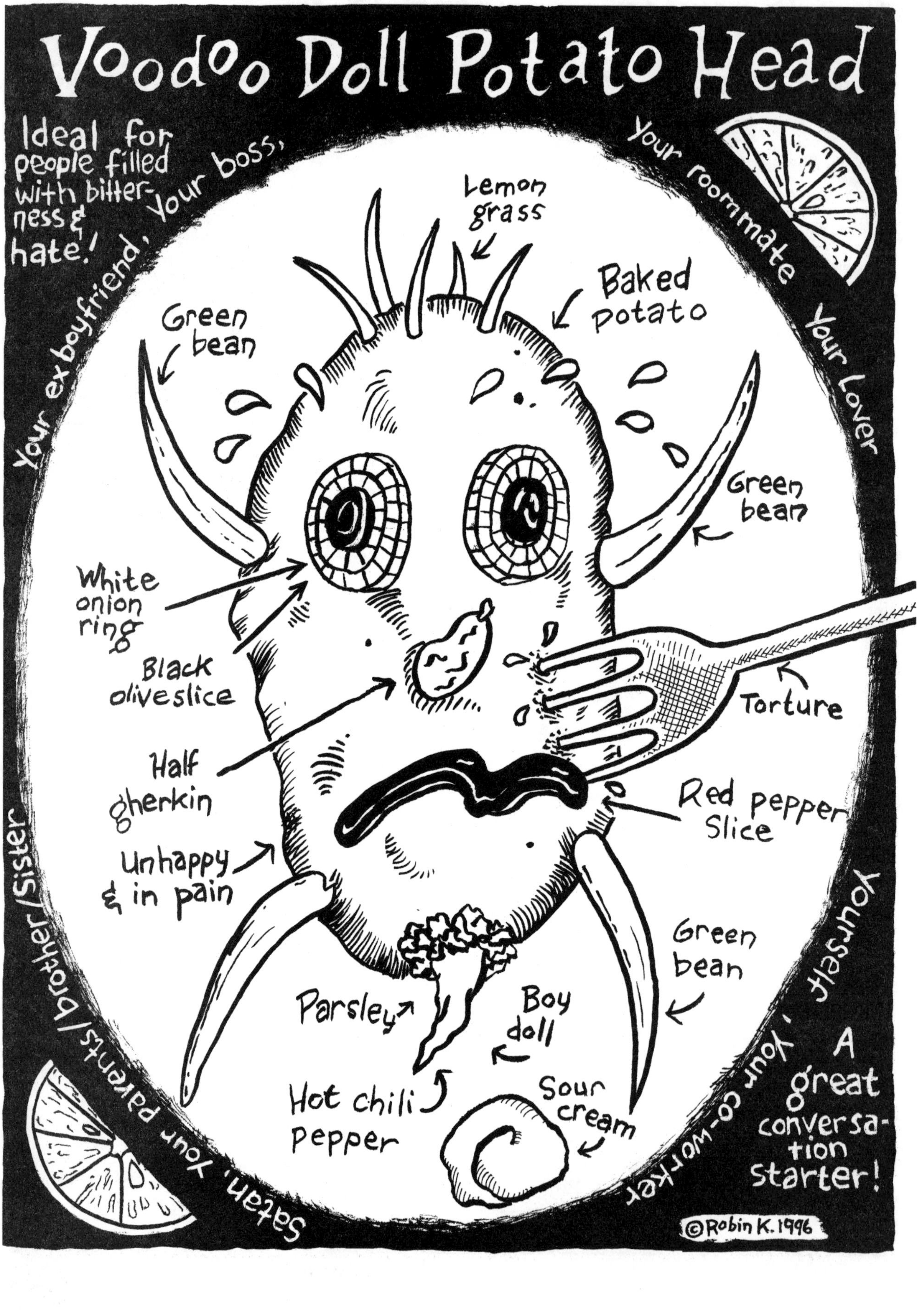

Voodoo Doll Potato Head
Ideal for people filled with bitterness & hate!
Your ex boyfriend, Your boss,
Your roommate Your Lover
Lemon grass
Baked potato
Green bean
Green bean
White onion ring
Black oliveslice
Half gherkin
Torture
Red pepper Slice
Unhappy & in pain
Green bean
Parsley
Boy doll
Hot chili pepper
Sour cream
Satan, your parents/brother/sister
Yourself, your co-worker
A great conversation starter!
©Robin K. 1996

Scalloped Potatoes

Just like Mom never made.

5 potatoes, peeled and thinly sliced

1 cup whipping cream

1 cup milk

2 tbsp. Dijon mustard

3 shallots, minced

1/4 cup fresh herbs (including at least 1/2 parsley, celery leaves, thyme, chervil, and oregano)

1 bay leaf

salt and pepper to taste

PREHEAT THE OVEN to 350°. In a saucepan over medium heat, add all the ingredients except for the potatoes and heat thoroughly, stirring occasionally. Do not bring it to a boil.

Grease a 9" x 13" baking pan and fan the potatoes onto it in even layers. You can make a funky potato design if you wish.

Remove the bay leaf from the liquid and gently pour it over the potatoes. The potatoes will swim in the liquid. Season to taste. Bake for 35-40 minutes uncovered.

Makes 6 servings.

CREAM MIXTURE

When you heat the milk and cream before adding it to the potatoes, it reduces the cooking time and intensifies the flavours of the herbs and shallots.

Spinach Gorgonzola Pie

This rich pie has never exploited Third World countries, and has never forgotten those pies that are less fortunate than itself.

1 Savoury Pie Crust, pg. 98

3 eggs

1 cup marscapone cheese (1 small container), at room temperature

2 cups spinach, chopped and blanched

3 1/2 oz. gorgonzola cheese, or to taste

1 onion, diced

3 cloves garlic, finely minced

2 tbsp. olive oil

1 tsp. oregano

1 tbsp. Dijon mustard

1 tsp. baking powder

salt and pepper to taste

START BY MAKING the pie crust dough and letting it rest. Preheat the oven to 400°.

To make 2 cups of blanched spinach, take 2-3 bunches of thoroughly washed spinach and chop them coarsely, then place them into a colander. Boil a moderate size pot of water and pour it over the chopped spinach. Let it sit and drain for a few minutes, then rinse it in cold water. Squeeze out as much juice as possible with your hands. If your squeezing is insufficient, you might end up with a mushy pie.

In a skillet over high heat, add the oil, onions, and a pinch of salt. Sauté for 3 minutes, then add the garlic, oregano, and spinach. Constantly stir and sauté for 3-5 minutes, or until the moisture in the spinach has mostly evaporated. Remove it from the heat and let cool. Use this cooling time to roll out the pie crust and place it into a 9-inch spring form pan, or a deep pie plate.

MR. & MRS. PARTY GAME

This party game may sound kind of lame, but it's actually really fun and quite cathartic. You need an even number of participants—at least 10—and the same number of pieces of paper. Someone will need to be the game master, who decides on a game theme (which he keeps secret), and then makes up theme-specific names. He writes each name on two pieces of paper, preceded by "Mr." and "Mrs."

For example, let's say the theme is sex. He might write "Mr. Suck" on one piece of paper, and "Mrs. Suck" on another. Then "Mr. Feltch" and "Mrs. Feltch," until all the pieces have names.

Everyone then stands in a circle and the game master throws the pieces of paper on the floor. Each person picks up a piece and yells

cont'd

In a mixing bowl, whisk the eggs with a pinch of salt. Add the marscapone cheese and mix thoroughly. Add the baking powder and mix thoroughly. Add the spinach mixture and stir together.

Break up the gorgonzola cheese into small pieces. Reserve a quarter of it, and mix the rest into the filling, then season to taste. Lots of pepper is nice in this pie.

Rub the Dijon mustard onto the bottom of the pie crust. Pour the filling into the crust and distribute the reserved gorgonzola on top.

Bake for 40-50 minutes, or until the crust edge is golden brown.

TIP FOR THE NOUVEAU RICHE: *Leave the foil wrapping on the cheese to show your society friends you can now afford real gorgonzola.*

PIE CRUST: *The recipe for savoury pie crust is for 2 bottom shells, or 1 top and bottom. Since you only need one shell for this recipe, you can freeze the remaining dough in a ball, or already rolled out and in a pie plate.*

out the name of his or her mate. Mrs. Pussy yells out, "Mr. Pussy, Mr. Pussy!" When Mrs. and Mr. Pussy are united, they sit down together. The last couple standing are the big losers.

Once you've played one round you'll want to play more. Really, we're not bulling you on this. You'll experience a sudden urge to throw your Pictionary in the garbage. You need to come up with new themes and new names for each round, the cruder the better. And don't be shy; you might get a date out of it.

Get rid of unwanted household items by giving them away as door or game prizes.

Savoury Pie Crust

Look, Mom, no lard!

3 cups all-purpose flour

1 cup butter, at room temperature

1 egg plus 1 tsp. vinegar, combined

4-6 tbsp. ice water (see note on pg. 28)

pinch of salt

SIFT THE FLOUR and salt into a mixing bowl and create a well in it. Cut in the butter with two knives or a pastry cutter. We'll say it again: Don't use your hands for this. When the butter is broken down into small pea-sized chunks add the egg, vinegar, and water. Quickly mix together with your hands and form into a ball. Refrigerate for 30 minutes before using.

Refer to the Short Pie Crust recipe, pg. 28, for techniques on rolling out pie crust.

Makes 1 top and 1 bottom crust.

Green Beans With Marjoram

A green bean adventure.

1 pound green beans

2 tsp. marjoram, freshly chopped

2 tbsp. olive oil

salt and pepper to taste

BLANCH THE GREEN BEANS for 3 to 5 minutes. Quickly strain and douse them in ice cold water, and then strain again to dry.

Heat a skillet over high heat and add the olive oil. Add the marjoram and the green beans and sauté for 5 minutes, stirring constantly to ensure even coating and cooking of the ingredients. Season to taste.

Serve immediately.

Makes 4 servings.

SAUTÉING BLANCHED VEGETABLES: *After blanching your vegetables, leave them to dry in a strainer before sautéing them. This will help prevent the skillet from spitting boiling oil onto you.*

A VALUABLE GUEST IS ONE WHO WILL **ENTERTAIN** AND BE **ENTERTAINED**

HEY, WHAT IS THIS?

YOU SAID WILLIAM S. BURROUGHS WOULD BE HERE

WELL, I DIDN'T HAVE TIME TO **MAKE** HIM

— BESIDES, IT WAS A **TRANSPARENT LIE**

I THOUGHT YOU'D HAVE SOME LOCAL CELEBRITIES, OR MAYBE JUST SOME PEOPLE WHO ARE **ALIVE**

I FEEL SO GYPPED

DON'T BE SUCH AN **INGRATE**

WE SPENT A LOT OF **TIME** AND **EFFORT** AND **MONEY** SO YOU COULD COME TO THIS GLAMOROUS CELEBRITY PARTY—AND PIERRE MADE A **CAKE**!

WHAT GLAMOROUS CELEBRITY PARTY?

WELL...

I GUESS IT'S NOT **REALLY** A CELEBRITY PARTY. IT'S MORE LIKE PLAYING WITH A LARGE **PAPER DOLL** SET!

A GIANT **PAPER DOLL** PARTY

THIS IS SO **NOWHERE**, MAN

I GOT THE IDEA FROM A **COMIC**

NOTHING EVER HAPPENS AROUND HERE. I JUST...I THOUGHT PEOPLE WOULD LIKE IT.

HOW **DISAPPOINTING**! I WAS HOPING TO HAVE SOME **ANIMATED** PARTY CHIT CHAT

COULDN'T YOU AT LEAST HAVE HAD PEOPLE IMPERSONATING CELEBRITIES OR SOMETHING

CARDBOARD CUTOUTS OF PEOPLE IMPERSONATING CELEBRITIES?

I CAN'T BELIEVE I TOOK THE NIGHT OFF WORK FOR **THIS**

RIP

RIP

RIP

COME OFF IT, YOU GUYS! IT'S BETTER THAN **T.V.**, RIGHT? **RIGHT?**

WELL, I GOTTA **GO**

KEEP THE STAR SHAPED PATÉ

YEAH, I'M GOING, TOO

LIFE'S TOO SHORT TO PLAY WITH PAPER DOLLS

WANNA COME, MARIA? THE X-FILES IS ON IN ½ AN HOUR

OKAY

YOU 2 SHOULD REALLY GET OUT MORE

Cooking with Weed*s*

Although we have heard that marijuana cultivation is the second largest economic industry in British Columbia, and that the *cannabis sativa* plant has been scientifically proven to aid medical conditions (high blood pressure, nausea, glaucoma, cancer and AIDS-related pain), and that one acre of hemp plants produces more usable paper fibres in one year than an acre of trees does in twenty—which, incidentally, require much less chemical processing than wood fibres—we'd like to remind you that the cannabis weed is *illegal.*

As law-abiding citizens, we feel it's important to stress that we've never actually tried any of the recipes in this chapter. No, Robin found these recipes in a secret drawer of an old roll-top desk she bought at an auction in Ottawa. Although Pierre says they look like they will work, these recipes are included for their entertainment value only. Trying them may result in a penalty of death (or is it a sense of well being?).

SPACE CADETS in OUTED Space
BY ROBIN SIGMUND KONSTÄFREUD 1997

WELL, THAT SO CALLED CELEBRITY PARTY WAS A TOTAL DISASTER

I WOULDN'T CALL IT A **TOTAL** DISASTER

I WOULD. EVERYTHING WENT WRONG, AND OUR FRIENDS DON'T WANT TO HANG AROUND WITH US ANYMORE.

THEY'LL GET OVER IT

NO, THEY WON'T. AND **WHY** THE **HELL** DID YOU INVITE JERRY GARCIA?

JERRY GARCIA? OF THE GRATEFUL DEAD? I DIDN'T INVITE **HIM**!

YOU DID SO!
HE WAS AT THE DOOR AND I HAD TO **KICK** HIM **OUT**

C'MON, PIERRE! **WHY WOULD** I INVITE HIM, KNOWING AS I DO ABOUT YOUR **FULL BLOWN HIPPIE PHOBIA**?

LOOK, ROBIN, I **KNOW** IT WAS **YOU** WHO INVITED HIM BE- CAUSE IT WAS **YOU** WHO **MADE** THOSE STUPID CARDBOARD CUT OUTS

YEAH, AND A LOT OF **THANKS** I GET, TOO

WELL, WHAT MADE YOU THINK PEOPLE WOULD ENJOY SUCH AN INANE PARTY?

I DUNNO...
I WOULD LIKE IT IF SOMEONE IN- VITED **ME** TO A PARTY LIKE THAT

ROBIN, WHEN ARE YOU GOING TO REAL- IZE THAT MOST PEOPLE **AREN'T** INTERESTED IN YOUR **OBSCURE** AND **INSULATED** HOB- BIES AND IDEAS?

WELL, IT'S JUST BECAUSE THEY **DON'T KNOW** WHAT THEY'RE **MISSING**
EVERYBODY COMPLAINS THEY'RE **BORED** ALL THE TIME AND THAT **NOTHING EVER HAPPENS.** I THOUGHT I COULD CREATE SOME EXCITEMENT

WITH **WHAT**? A PAPER DOLL PARTY AND JERRY GARCIA?

WELL, YEAH. AND **NEVER MIND** JER- RY GARCIA, WHAT HAPPENED TO THAT DAN CLOWES CUT OUT I MADE?
HUH? HUH?

I DON'T EVEN **KNOW** WHO THAT IS

GEEZ, GET **WITH** IT, PIERRE. **DAN CLOWES**–CREATOR OF AMERICA'S **MOST LOVED** COMIC MAGAZINE

YOU MEAN **ROBIN'S** MOST LOVED COMIC MAGAZINE

YEAH, WHATEVER

ANYWAY, I SPENT A LOT OF **TIME** MAKING THE CLOWES CUT OUT AND HE WAS GOING TO BE MY **FAVOURITE** GUEST, SO **WHERE WAS HE?**

MEANWHILE, IN THE BASEMENT...
SLOPPY AMATEURS

GEE, ROBIN, I DON'T KNOW. MAYBE YOU WERE SO **BUSY** MAKING THE **GARCIA** CUT OUT YOU DIDN'T GET **AROUND** TO CLOWES

FOR THE LAST TIME, **I DID NOT MAKE** A JERRY GARCIA CUT OUT. I DON'T KNOW WHAT YOU'RE TALKING ABOUT

JERRY GARCIA! **JERRY GARCIA** AT OUR FRONT DOOR CLAIMING HE'S **JESUS CHRIST**

WELL, YOU MUST HAVE IMAGINED IT ALL

I DID **NOT!** ASK THE CHICKEN. SHE WAS **THERE**

THE CHICKEN?! ASK THE **CHICKEN!**
YOU WANNA KNOW WHAT I THINK?

NO

I THINK YOU'RE A **CLOSET HIPPIE**

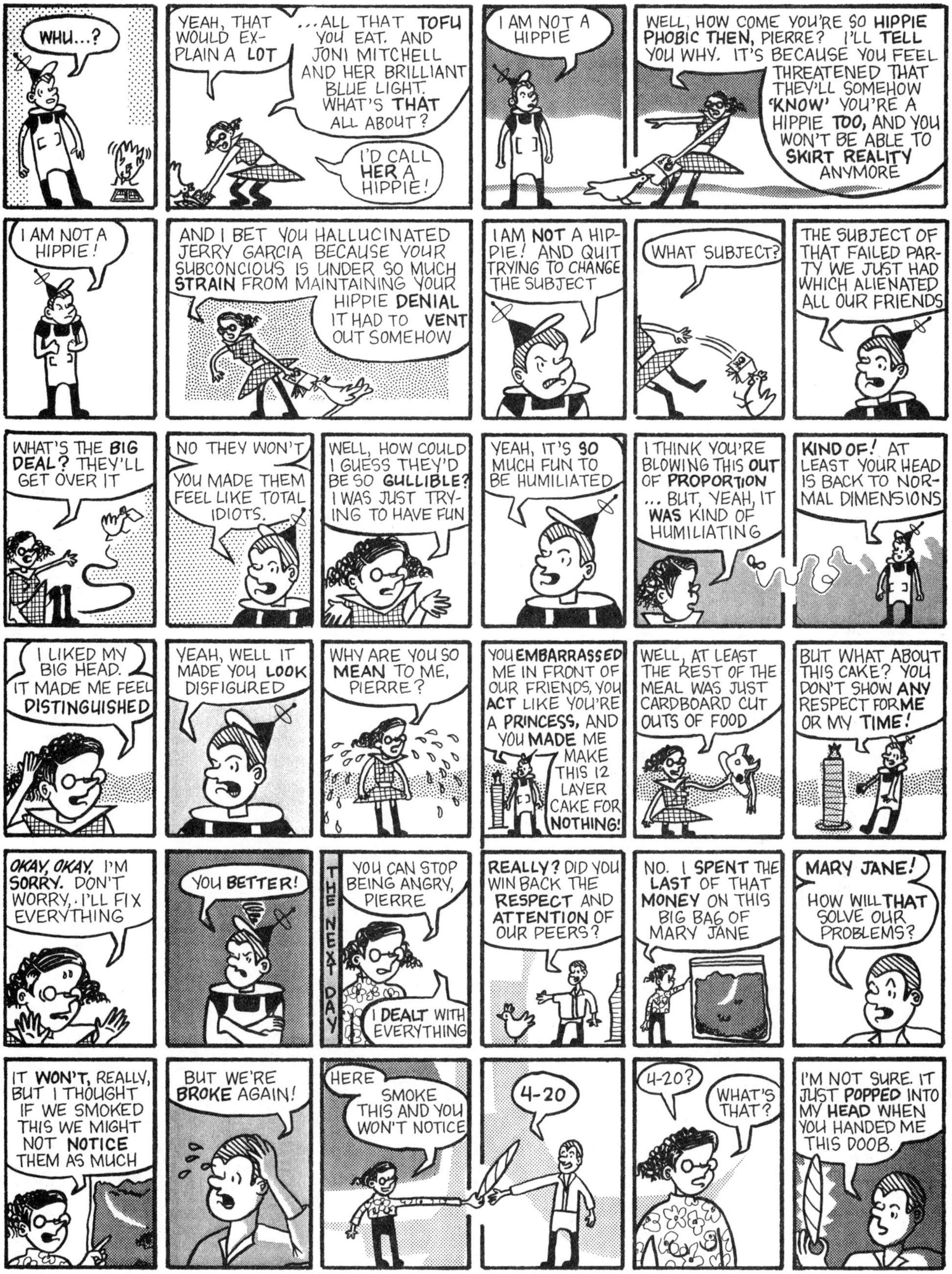
WHU...?
YEAH, THAT WOULD EXPLAIN A LOT
...ALL THAT TOFU YOU EAT. AND JONI MITCHELL AND HER BRILLIANT BLUE LIGHT. WHAT'S THAT ALL ABOUT?
I'D CALL HER A HIPPIE!
I AM NOT A HIPPIE
WELL, HOW COME YOU'RE SO HIPPIE PHOBIC THEN, PIERRE? I'LL TELL YOU WHY. IT'S BECAUSE YOU FEEL THREATENED THAT THEY'LL SOMEHOW 'KNOW' YOU'RE A HIPPIE TOO, AND YOU WON'T BE ABLE TO SKIRT REALITY ANYMORE
I AM NOT A HIPPIE!
AND I BET YOU HALLUCINATED JERRY GARCIA BECAUSE YOUR SUBCONCIOUS IS UNDER SO MUCH STRAIN FROM MAINTAINING YOUR HIPPIE DENIAL IT HAD TO VENT OUT SOMEHOW
I AM NOT A HIPPIE! AND QUIT TRYING TO CHANGE THE SUBJECT
WHAT SUBJECT?
THE SUBJECT OF THAT FAILED PARTY WE JUST HAD WHICH ALIENATED ALL OUR FRIENDS
WHAT'S THE BIG DEAL? THEY'LL GET OVER IT
NO THEY WON'T
YOU MADE THEM FEEL LIKE TOTAL IDIOTS.
WELL, HOW COULD I GUESS THEY'D BE SO GULLIBLE? I WAS JUST TRYING TO HAVE FUN
YEAH, IT'S SO MUCH FUN TO BE HUMILIATED
I THINK YOU'RE BLOWING THIS OUT OF PROPORTION ... BUT, YEAH, IT WAS KIND OF HUMILIATING
KIND OF! AT LEAST YOUR HEAD IS BACK TO NORMAL DIMENSIONS
I LIKED MY BIG HEAD. IT MADE ME FEEL DISTINGUISHED
YEAH, WELL IT MADE YOU LOOK DISFIGURED
WHY ARE YOU SO MEAN TO ME, PIERRE?
YOU EMBARRASSED ME IN FRONT OF OUR FRIENDS, YOU ACT LIKE YOU'RE A PRINCESS, AND YOU MADE ME MAKE THIS 12 LAYER CAKE FOR NOTHING!
WELL, AT LEAST THE REST OF THE MEAL WAS JUST CARDBOARD CUT OUTS OF FOOD
BUT WHAT ABOUT THIS CAKE? YOU DON'T SHOW ANY RESPECT FOR ME OR MY TIME!
OKAY, OKAY, I'M SORRY. DON'T WORRY, I'LL FIX EVERYTHING
YOU BETTER!
THE NEXT DAY
YOU CAN STOP BEING ANGRY, PIERRE
I DEALT WITH EVERYTHING
REALLY? DID YOU WIN BACK THE RESPECT AND ATTENTION OF OUR PEERS?
NO. I SPENT THE LAST OF THAT MONEY ON THIS BIG BAG OF MARY JANE
MARY JANE!
HOW WILL THAT SOLVE OUR PROBLEMS?
IT WON'T, REALLY, BUT I THOUGHT IF WE SMOKED THIS WE MIGHT NOT NOTICE THEM AS MUCH
BUT WE'RE BROKE AGAIN!
HERE
SMOKE THIS AND YOU WON'T NOTICE
4-20
4-20?
WHAT'S THAT?
I'M NOT SURE. IT JUST POPPED INTO MY HEAD WHEN YOU HANDED ME THIS DOOB.

MAYBE YOU COULD SELL MORE COMICS TO THAT GUY

AHEM! WELL...YEAH
I KIND OF LIED ABOUT THAT

I KNEW IT!
WHERE DID ALL THAT MONEY COME FROM?

WHAT REALLY HAPPENED IS THAT GUY DID BUY THE LAST COPY, BUT HE INSTANTLY RIPPED IT UP TO MAKE PAPER BOATS

HE GAVE YOU ALL THAT MONEY FOR PAPER BOAT MATERIAL?

NO. HE GAVE ME 1 DOLLAR, WHICH I THEN SPENT ON A WINNING SCRATCH AND WIN TICKET

SOB
WHY DID YOU LIE TO ME?

WELL, FOR ONE THING I DIDN'T WANT TO ADMIT I HAD FALLEN OFF THE SCRATCH AND WIN WAGON... AND ALSO IT OCCURRED TO ME THAT MAYBE MAINTAINING THE PRETEXT OF SUCCESS IS JUST AS GOOD AS ACTUAL SUCCESS

THE PRETEXT... IS IT?

ALMOST
AND IT'S A LOT LESS WORK!

AND LESS MONEY, TOO, ALL WE HAVE IS THIS CARDBOARD FOOD

AND THIS CAKE
MMM... 12 LAYER CAKE

ONE WEEK LATER

GROOVY NEWS, MAN! I GOT PROMOTED AT 'TOAST 'R' US'!
OUR MONEY PROBLEMS ARE SOLVED

GOOD, 'CAUSE I'M SO SICK OF THIS CAKE

YEAH, I GOT PROMOTED TO HEMP FOOD RESEARCHER

HEMP FOOoo -AHHghAH!- WHAT HAPPENED TO YOUR HAIR?

NOTHING.
I'M GROWING IT

IT'S HIPPIE HAIR!

NO, IT'S NOT.
I JUST WANT A NEW LOOK
OK?

AND YOU SAID 'GROOVY'!

NO, I DIDN'T

YES, YOU DID
WHEN YOU CAME IN THE DOOR YOU SAID "GROOVY NEWS, MAN"

NO, I DIDN'T

YES, YOU DID! AND WHAT'S WITH THIS HEMP FOOD RESEARCH JOB?
THAT'S A HIPPIE JOB!

NO, IT'S NOT. 'TOAST 'R' US' JUST WANTS TO KEEP WITH THE TIMES. YOU KNOW, GET NOW, GET WITH IT!

ONLY A HIPPIE WOULD TRY TO EAT POT

LISTEN, EDIBLE HEMP PRODUCTS ARE A GOOD SOURCE OF ESSENTIAL FATTY ACIDS THAT OUR BODIES CAN'T PRODUCE, SUCH AS AMINO 8.
ALSO, HEMP PLANTS ARE FAST AND EASY TO GROW, AND THEIR FIBERS ARE USABLE FOR THE MANUFACTURE OF PAPER, TEXTILES AND FUEL

YOU REALLY ARE A HIPPIE!

IT'S THE WAVE OF THE FUTURE. IT'S A MIRACLE PLANT AND IT'S A WEED!

OH NO! NOW YOU'LL BE DOING TIE DYE IN THE BATHTUB

MELLOW OUT, ROBIN. OPEN THE DOOR TO THE LOVE AND GOODNESS OF THE UNIVERSE AND YOU WILL FIND INNER PEACE.
IT'S SO MIND EXPANDING!
I'LL MAKE YOU SOME STINGING NETTLE TEA AND WE CAN DO YOGA!

HAVE YOU SEEN MY BIRKENSTOCKS
OOOOH I FEEL ALL SQUEAMISH...

Hempy Homous

Makes a hippie staple hipper.

2 1/2 cups cooked garbanzo beans

1/4 cup sesame seeds

2 cloves garlic, crushed

juice of one lemon

1 tbsp. hemp seed oil

cayenne pepper to taste

1 tbsp. yoghurt (optional)

ROAST THE SESAME SEEDS in a dry skillet over high heat, shaking constantly. Put them in the food processor (the one you still haven't returned to your neighbour) and turn it onto high speed. With the processor still on, add the garlic and the lemon juice, then gradually add the garbanzo beans, hemp seed oil, cayenne pepper, and optional yoghurt. (If you are not using hemp seed oil, try extra virgin olive oil.) Purée until the consistency is uniform.

Serve with pita bread or crustini.

Makes about 2 cups.

THE AMERICAN LEGACY

People can't seem to decide whether the hemp plant should be legal or not, even though the industrial hemp plant contains only a negligible amount of THC. There is much government bureaucracy surrounding its research and cultivation, resulting in confusion and conflicting information within the industry. Also, because hemp fibres make paper, fuel, fabrics, and excellent ropes, certain parties concerned with the wood pulp, paper, and petro-chemical industries are not anxious to see industrial hemp as a common crop.

All we can say is that George Washington was a hemp farmer long before those DuPonts showed up. So look out—the next thing you know they'll be busting Granny for growing poppies in her yard!

Modern research has shown that hemp seeds are highly nutritious because they contain essential fatty acids. There are a variety of hemp seed-based food products on the market today, including oil, flour, prefab cookie dough, energy bars, hemp coffee, and mock cheese. These foods are available in many hemp shops, some health food stores, and there was even some of that cheese at the local Safeway.

Reports from the Scrambled Brains *Laboratory on the hemp palatability level were not 100 percent favourable. The seeds of the hemp plant were found to be surrounded with tough shell-like husks which are difficult to remove, and tend to get stuck between your teeth. Also, the flour was discovered to have a very short shelf life, as the hemp seed germ, where the fatty acids live, can go rancid easily.*

As any desperate stoner knows, hemp seeds do not contain tetrahydrocan-nabinol (that's what gets you "high"—hereafter known as THC). At present it is illegal to sell hemp

cont'd

Mushroom and Millet Surprise

An astonishing spread.

1/2 cup millet

1 1/2 cups vegetable broth

1 small onion, diced

3 cloves garlic, minced

1 pound button mushrooms, whole

2 tbsp. flour

1 tbsp. cooking oil

2 tbsp. hemp seed oil

1 tsp. soy sauce

salt and pepper to taste

START BY COOKING THE MILLET in the vegetable broth in a covered pot over low heat for 30 minutes. Let cool.

Put the cooking oil in a large skillet over medium high heat, and sauté onions and mushrooms with a pinch of salt for 5 minutes. Sprinkle flour into the skillet and stir. Reduce to low heat and cook for another 5 minutes, stirring occasionally. Let cool.

In a food processor, purée the mushroom mixture. Add the millet, hemp seed oil, soy sauce, season to taste, and purée to a fine paste.

Serve chilled with crackers, bread or crudités.

Makes about 2 1/2 cups.

Purple Potato and Sundried Tomato Salad

An uppity gourmet dish.

6 cups purple potatoes, cut into cubes and cooked

2 tbsp. sundried tomatoes, rehydrated and finely chopped

1 bunch green onions, chopped

1 clove garlic, finely minced

1 tsp. dill

3 tbsp. balsamic vinegar

1 tsp. Dijon mustard

1/4 cup roasted bell peppers, cut into small pieces

1/4 cup hemp seed oil

salt and pepper to taste

IN A BOWL, mix the vinegar, Dijon mustard, garlic, dill, and sundried tomatoes. Whisk in the hemp seed oil and add the purple potatoes. Toss, add the green onions and bell peppers, and toss again. Salt and pepper to taste.

Makes 6 portions.

WHAT! PURPLE POTATOES?: *Purple potatoes are like red potatoes, except they're purple inside and out. They're nothing new. Ask your granny, and if she knows anything at all about potatoes she will tell you it's a heritage strain. They're available in some farmers' markets, but they're hard to find, so you may have to grow your own.*

seeds which are unsterilized, although the plants these seeds would produce would be of the industrial variety and contain very little THC. Some hemp researchers believe that this sterilization process adversely affects the nutritional value of the seed.

THE HEMP SEED OIL SUPPLEMENT

Of all the hemp seed food products tested at the Scrambled Brains Laboratory, the cold-pressed oil was found to be the most palatable. Two tablespoons daily are recommended for good health. The oil should be bought freshly pressed and kept in the freezer after opening. This dark-green-coloured oil has an earthy flavour that is slightly reminiscent of sesame seeds and is quite nice on a salad. It cannot be used as a cooking oil since heat and light will spoil it. At present it costs about $20 CDN for 250 millilitres (8.5 ounces).

Here are some salad dressings to start you off. Whisk these ingredients together in order of appearance.

CREAMY DRESSINGS

Wasabi Dressing

1/2 cup mayonnaise

juice of 1/2 lemon

1 tbsp. wasabi paste

Avocado Dressing

1 ripe avocado

juice of 1/2 lemon

1/4 cup plain yoghurt

1 tsp. fresh cilantro, chopped

1 clove garlic, minced

1 tsp. olive oil

3 tsp. water

pinch of chili pepper

Whipless Wonder

1 cup mayonnaise

1 tbsp. sugar

2 tbsp. vinegar

Salad is Good

In the Canada Food Guide, the government tells us to eat a cup of salad every day. Obey the government.

Salads are easy to make and the possibilities of different vegetable combinations are virtually limitless, but it should go without saying that the freshest salad is the best salad, so buy ingredients that are in season.

Start with greens such as lettuce, spinach, cabbage, and endive, and then get fancier with arugula, mustard greens, watercress, and chard. Don't laugh, but some edible flowers are yummy: pansies, calendulas, and the well-known nasturtium flower and its leaves.

Many things grow wild which you can eat for free, such as chickweed, land cress, and dandelion leaves.

The list of possible salad ingredients grows and grows. With the current genetic criss-cross hoopla, there are now enough new varieties of vegetable hybrids to satisfy every taste and fantasy. Yes, we have been liberated from the tyranny of iceberg lettuce!

The Best Dressed Award

Gone with the iceberg lettuce are the days of bottled salad dressing. Modern cooks make their own and call it vinaigrette. Why? Because it's quick, easy, and economical. 1 part vinegar to 3 parts oil, salt, and pepper, and voilà, vinaigrette! What could be simpler? Zest up your vinaigrette with mustard, herbs, and/or lemon. For a creamy dressing start with mayonnaise, yoghurt, or sour cream (or *crème fraîche*), and add herbs, spices, and/or garlic. If your creamy dressing is too thick, you can dilute it with water, milk, or lemon juice. Keep it simple and try to use ingredients you have on hand.

Oils

Many types of oils are tasty in salads. Extra virgin olive oil is the undisputed queen of the salad bowl. Nut oils are a bit pricier but their flavours are extremely concentrated, so you only need to use a little bit. Roast sesame oil, for example, is not too expensive. These oils can be diluted with a lighter, more affordable oil such as sunflower or canola oil.

Much research has been done on the health benefits of certain oils in your diet, mainly flax seed oil and hemp seed oil, because they contain essential fatty acids that cannot be produced by the human body. These fatty acids help our bodies store energy and stay healthy.

Natural food stores normally carry these oils. Look for the ones that say "unrefined" and "cold-pressed." Because of their sensitive nature, these oils should be consumed uncooked to prevent rancidity. Heating them kills their nutrients, so what better way to consume them than on a salad?

Vinegars

A wide variety of vinegars are readily available on the market: plain white vinegar, cider vinegar, red and white and sherry wine vinegars, balsamic vinegar, and rice vinegar. Some are preseasoned, fruity, or herbed. You can make your own flavoured vinegars by putting your favourite ingredient and any type of basic vinegar into an airtight bottle. Let it sit for at least 6 weeks. Use herbs, fruit—whatever. You can strain it before use, but it's not necessary. It's more fun than glue gun art and tastes better too.

Many books have been written about salads, dressings, and infusions. All we are sure of is that you must eat 1 cup of salad a day to avoid Canada Food Guide officials at your door asking embarrassing personal questions.

VINAIGRETTES

Balsamic Vinaigrette

2 tbsp. balsamic vinegar

1 tbsp. fresh basil, chopped

1 tbsp. fresh parsley, chopped

1 small shallot

1 clove garlic, minced

1 tsp. Dijon mustard

1/4 cup salad oil

1/4 cup olive oil

salt and pepper to taste

Orange Vinaigrette

juice of 1 orange

1 tbsp. apple cider vinegar

pinch of minced garlic

1 tbsp. fresh basil, chopped

1 tsp. Dijon mustard

1/4 cup salad oil

1 tbsp. olive oil

salt and pepper to taste

Sesame Ginger Vinaigrette

1 tbsp. rice vinegar

1/2 tbsp. brown sugar

1 tsp. soy sauce

1 tsp. fresh ginger, minced

1/4 cup salad oil

1 tbsp. sesame oil

THC Infusion

An illusion allusion.

1/2 cup high quality extra virgin olive oil

2-4 tbsp. of kick-ass bud, the best you can get

1 sprig of fresh rosemary (optional)

PLACE THE BUD and optional rosemary in an airtight jar and pour the oil over it. Make sure the oil covers the bud and rosemary completely. Tightly seal the jar and store it in a cool, dark place (do not refrigerate). Let sit for at least 6 weeks.

After 6 weeks, strain the oil through a cheesecloth to remove the plant goop. The infusion will keep indefinitely, as long as it is stored as described.

Makes 1/2 cup.

I TINCT SOMETHING'S IN MY MARTINI: *The infusion method can also be used to make tinctures by substituting vodka or other kinds of alcohol for the oil. Leave out the rosemary.*

Miró Dip

Everyone knows this dip, but no one knows what it's called. So we just made up the name.

4 tbsp. THC Infusion

1 tbsp. balsamic vinegar

1 clove garlic, in thin slivers

IN A SMALL shallow side dish, place the garlic slivers and pour the THC infusion oil over them. Pour the vinegar on top. Doesn't it look just like a painting by the famous surrealist Joan Miró? For an even more Miróesque effect, splash the vinegar a bit when adding it.

This is a dip for focaccia bread, so serve it with focaccia bread.

Makes 2 servings.

FEEDING WEED TO FAMILY AND FRIENDS: *Never, ever, ever, ever, ever feed weed to someone who is not aware they are eating weed. If you bring something like a Ginger and Mary Jane Bread to a party, make sure it is clearly labelled. Failure to follow this advice could result in vomit and loss of friends.*

Space Butter

It gets you spaced.

22 cups weed "shake" (10 oz.)
5 cups butter (2 1/2 lbs.)

COOKING TIME

Many people believe the longer you cook weed, the more THC it will render. This is not true. Most of the THC comes out during the first 20-25 minutes of cooking. After that you are only extracting other chemical components that aren't so good for you.

COOKING TEMPERATURE

It is said that THC loses some potency when exposed to extreme heat, so melt the butter slowly and keep it on a gentle simmer.

MELT THE BUTTER in a large, heavy-bottomed cooking pot. Add the shake a couple of handfuls at a time, allowing the leaves to soak up the butter. A potato masher is handy for tamping down the leaves. At this point you may want to open the window to get the odd and incriminating odours out of the house. Simmer over a very low temperature for not more than 25 minutes.

Let it cool and sit overnight in the fridge or on the porch if the weather is not warm.

In the morning slowly remelt the butter until it is more or less liquid again. Place a colander or strainer in a large mixing bowl, and line it with a large piece of cheesecloth.

In small batches, pour the butter and leaves into the strainer and squeeze out the butter with the cheesecloth. This will ensure minimal waste of the sacred butter. It is not suggested that you do anything with the spent weed leaves besides throw them away.

When cool, the butter will have the consistency and texture of butter that has melted and rehardened. For creamy space butter, re-whip it with a mixer or whisk.

Freeze what you don't use immediately.

Makes around 3 cups.

THC: THE CHUBBY CHASER: *THC likes to party, so if it doesn't have fatty food or alcohol to play with, it won't be coaxed out of the marijuana plant. The THC is contained in the plant's resins, which are not water soluble; therefore, in order to prepare marijuana for consumption, it must first be mixed with alcohol or some kind of fat and allowed to sit for a while so it may render the THC.*

Mary Jane's Faux Truffles

Dedicated to Pot Brownie Mary.

1 cup cocoa

1 cup icing sugar

1/2 cup butter, at room temperature

1/2 cup space butter, at room temperature

2 oz. flavoured liqueur (see sidebar)

about 1/2 cup cocoa, or icing sugar, or coconut, or chocolate
  vermicelli, or roasted nuts for rolling

FIRST, BEAT THE BUTTERS together with a mixer on high speed
until they are perfectly soft and uniform. Combine the cocoa with
the sugar and whip it into the butter in small increments. Dribble
in a small bit of liqueur when the mix becomes too dry to blend
well (be conservative with your dribble amounts; if you add too
much, the mix will get too soft). Control the mixer speed and use a
rubber spatula to scrape the sides of the bowl.

Put the faux truffle mix in the freezer for 15 to 20 minutes, or until
it is firm. Roll it into 1-inch balls. A melon baller is the perfect tool
for this, but for those who are melon baller deprived, try a
teaspoon. The less you manipulate the balls with your hands the
better, because the heat from your hands will soften them and
make them hard to handle.

As each ball is formed, roll it immediately in the coating of your
choice.

Keep these frozen until about 10 minutes before you eat them.

Makes 48 truffles.

FLAVOUR VARIATIONS

*The combinations of liqueur
and truffle coatings are
infinite. Amaretto and
toasted almond slivers are
good. Other people may
prefer cointreau and icing
sugar.*

*You can also add endless
flavours to your truffles by
adding items such as 2
tablespoons of orange zest,
or 2 tablespoons of minced
ginger. Divide the truffle
mix and add different
ingredients to make a
variety of flavours from a
single batch.*

TEETOTALLERS

*If you do not consume
alcohol, you can substitute 1
teaspoon vanilla extract plus
however much water or milk
or coffee you need to attain
the right consistency.*

KITCHEN SAFETY

*Never stick your tongue in
the beaters while the mixer
is on.*

PIERRE AND THE MAN

LOCAL NITWIT

Once, a neighbour of Robin and Pierre stopped by to inform them she had joined the neighbourhood "Pot Watch," a group of people who roamed the area looking for hemp plants, then snitched on the cultivators to local police. Because they had 6 hemp plants growing in the garden of their enclosed back yard, this sort of worried them.

One day late in summer they were sitting in the garden with the gate open and this same neighbour poked her head in to chat. What could they do but invite her in for tea?

They asked how the neighbourhood Pot Watch was doing and she replied it was going well. "I can spot a plant a mile off!" she claimed.

The conversation must have been riveting, for she could see all 6 plants from her seat and identified none of them.

Once again reassured of the incompetence of their local vigilantes, Robin and Pierre slept well for the rest of the harvest season.

COOKING WITH WEED$

Space Stacks

Totally orbital.

2 cups sugar

6 tbsp. cocoa

1/2 cup space butter

1/2 cup milk

1 tsp. pure vanilla extract

1 1/2 cups shredded coconut

3 cups instant oats

pinch of salt

IN A SAUCEPAN OVER medium high heat, combine the sugar, cocoa, space butter, milk, and the pinch of salt. Bring to a boil, stirring occasionally, for 3-5 minutes. Remove from heat and add vanilla extract, oats, and coconut. Stir it all together and spoon out golf ball-sized portions onto a piece of parchment or wax paper.

Let cool for an hour before eating.

Refrigerate or freeze unconsumed space stacks.

Makes 24 stacks.

DEALING WITH THE MUNCHIES: *Many people experience a strong desire to eat when under the influence of weed. To avoid a vicious circle (ending in paranoia), munch only things that do not contain weed.*

MONITORING WEED CONSUMPTION: *Everyone will have a different tolerance level of, and reaction to, weed, so it is a good idea to start with a small portion, then wait about an hour to see how you feel before going for seconds.*

PERSUASION

PIERRE, DESPERATE TIMES CALL FOR DESPERATE MEASURES...

WHAT DO YOU MEAN?

YOU'LL HAVE TO GO OUT AND **SELL** THE SCHMOOGLYBOOGLE FOR FOOD MONEY

GEEZ, ROBIN! WHY DON'T YOU JUST GO TO WELFARE?

I'M TOO **PROUD**

I'D **RATHER** SELL OUR PERSONAL BELONGINGS

-AND I FIGURED OUT THAT THE ONLY THINGS WE OWN OF **ANY VALUE** ARE THAT BAG OF WEED, MY COMIC BOOK COLLECTION, AND **THIS** SCHMOOGLYBOOGLE

AND SINCE THOSE THINGS ARE ACTUALLY **MINE**, AND I'LL BE SHARING THE MONEY WITH **YOU**, IT SHOULD BE YOU WHO DOES THE WORK OF SELLING THEM

BUT IT'S AN **ATOMIC EXPLOSIVE DEVICE!**

WELL, IF YOU DON'T DO IT I'LL BE **FORCED** TO **EAT** THE CHICKEN

OKAY!

-I'LL DO IT-

-BUT **ONLY** TO SAVE THE LIFE OF THAT INNOCENT CHICKEN

Pot Kookies

The name says it all.

1/2 cup granulated sugar

1/3 cup packed brown sugar

1/2 cup space butter

1 egg

1 tsp. pure vanilla extract

1 1/3 cups all purpose flour

1/2 tsp. baking soda

1/2 tsp. salt

1 cup chocolate chips

1/2 cup pecans, chopped

1/4 cup toasted hemp seeds (optional)

1/2 cup raisins (optional)

PREHEAT OVEN to 350°.

Sift the flour, baking soda, and salt into a bowl. In another bowl, cream the butter and sugar with an electric mixer until the sugar has completely dissolved and the butter is creamy with no grit. (This takes some time but it is the secret of an exceptional cookie.) Add the egg and vanilla and beat until fluffy. With your electric mixer on low speed, add the flour mix in increments. With a wooden spoon, mix in the chocolate chips, pecans, and optional toasted hemp seeds and raisins.

Scoop teaspoon-sized chunks of dough onto a greased baking sheet, about 2 inches apart. Bake for 8-12 minutes, or until they become a light brownish green. Cooking time depends on your oven, so keep a close eye on the first couple of batches until you get the timing down.

Makes 3 dozen kookies.

COOKING TIME: *Don't be fooled when baking kookies. They're just like cookies and crisp when cooling.*

COOKING WITH WEED$

Ginger and Mary Jane Bread

Go ask Alice.

1 1/2 cups flour

1 cup dark brown sugar

1 1/2 tsp. ground cloves

1 1/2 tsp. ground cinnamon

1 1/2 tsp. ground cardoman seed

3/4 cup dark molasses

1/2 cup butter, melted

3 eggs, beaten

1/3 cup minced fresh ginger

2 1/2 cups low-grade weed bud (1 ounce), ground to a powder in your coffee grinder or food processor

1 1/2 tsp. baking soda

3/4 cup hot water

1 tsp. orange zest

pinch of salt

PREHEAT OVEN to 325°.

In a bowl, sift together the flour, weed bud, sugar, and spices with a pinch of salt.

In a large mixing bowl combine the molasses, melted butter, beaten eggs, ginger, and orange zest. With a wooden spoon mix the dry ingredients with the wet, adding them in increments.

In a small bowl or cup, dissolve the baking soda in the hot water, then vigorously stir it into the cake mix. Pour it into a 9″ x 12″ baking pan and bake for 35-40 minutes, or until the cake edge leaves the side of the pan.

Makes one cake.

TRUE OR FALSE

There's a rumour going around that the slang word "toke" (meaning a puff from a marijuana cigarette) originated from Alice B. Toklas, the lover of Gertrude Stein and a writer of cookbooks. In The Alice B. Toklas Cookbook, *published in 1954, she included a recipe for "Hashish Fudge," which had* cannibis sativa *as its principal ingredient. Alice B. later claimed that she didn't know what* cannabis sativa *was, and that she had had friends submit recipes for her book which she never examined before sending to her publishers, who edited the recipe out of the American edition. Her British editor included the recipe in the first printing of the British edition, some said as a publicity stunt, others said as an exercise in free speech. Today, all editions of her book include this infamous recipe, resulting in a perhaps not-so-true stoner reputation for Alice B.*

TO BE CONTINUED...

Chicken Gatcân'sa

Killing 1 bird for 1 stone.

1 dead chicken, cut into cubes

10 cups water

1 tbsp. tamarind paste

1 bunch of green onions, chopped

1 big marijuana bud

salt and pepper to taste

PLACE THE CHICKEN CUBES into a large pot with the water and salt and pepper and bring to a boil, then reduce it to simmer for 30-40 minutes.

In a small bowl, dissolve the tamarind paste with some liquid from the pot, then add it and the bud to the stew. Cook for another 20 minutes. Season to taste and serve over steamed rice with green onions.

Makes 4 servings.

TAMARIND PASTE: *The tamarind fruit—also known as Indian date—grows in tropical areas of the Eastern hemisphere and is made into a paste that is widely used in Indian and Asian cuisines, especially in chutneys and broths. It has a bittersweet flavour with a hint of lemon. In a pinch you can substitute lemon for tamarind paste, but it's not as good. Here in the West, thousands of people consume tamarind paste every day without even knowing it. It's in HP Sauce!*

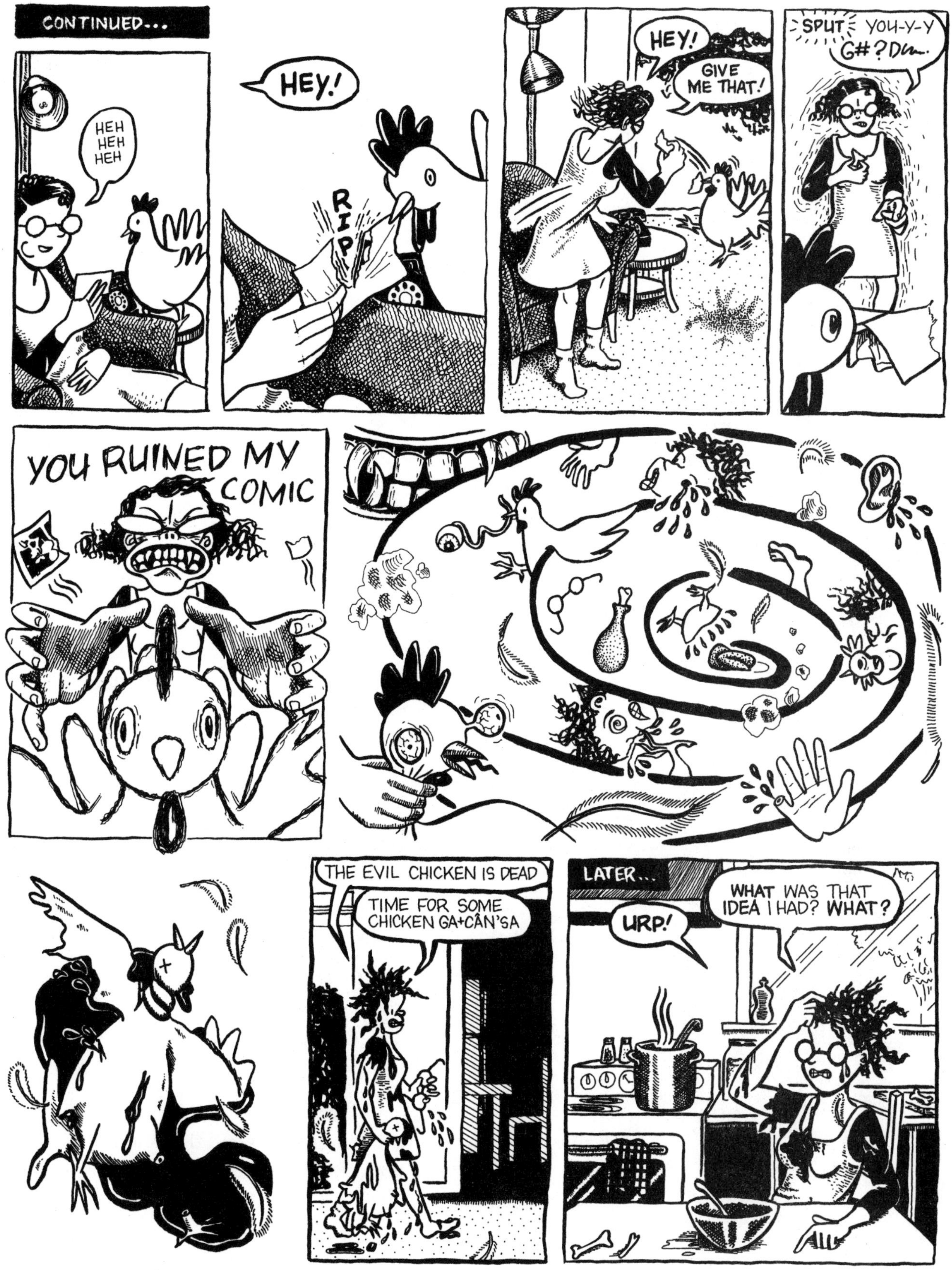
CONTINUED...
HEH HEH HEH
HEY!
RIP
HEY!
GIVE ME THAT!
SPUT YOU-Y-Y G#?D
YOU RUINED MY COMIC
THE EVIL CHICKEN IS DEAD
TIME FOR SOME CHICKEN GA+CÂN'SA
LATER...
URP!
WHAT WAS THAT IDEA I HAD? WHAT?

Majun

A classic stoner treat from exotic Eastern lands.

4 1/4 cups low-grade weed buds

2 tbsp. butter at room temperature

1 cup honey

1 1/2 tbsp. caraway seeds

2 1/2 tsp. speculaas spice (see pg. 51)

1 cup roasted almond slivers, or nut of choice

1 tsp. baking soda

PICK OUT the stems and twigs from the weed bud. Place the cleaned weed and the butter into a food processor and combine until the butter is integrated. Do not grind it into a powder, leave it fairly coarse. Put it into an airtight container and let it sulk for a few hours or overnight. This step is necessary for good results.

In a cast-iron skillet, gradually heat the honey, stirring occasionally until it reaches 280°. Use a candy thermometer to measure the temperature. If you don't have a candy thermometer you can't make this recipe, so consider buying one.

Once the honey has reached 280°, stir in the caraway seeds, speculaas, and almonds, and heat until the candy thermometer registers 300°, no more, no less. (We believe this is called the "hard crack" stage.) Remove it from the heat and quickly stir in the sulking weed. Quick, quick. Add the baking soda and stir it in. It will foam up and make the candy more dandy.

Quickly spread the mixture onto a pre-greased baking sheet and, with your hands, form into a rectangular shape, roughly 8" x 10" and about 1/4-inch thick. You gotta act fast because the candy is hardening as we speak. You should also score the candy with a sharp knife into 1 1/2-inch square portions.

Let it finish cooling and hardening for an hour, then cut into portions along the scored lines. Freeze what you don't eat.

Makes 40 pieces.

Bre-X Gold Bars

They're good enough to lose your shirt over.

1 Majun recipe, pg. 122

4-6 sheets edible gold leaf or,

1 jar edible gold dust and new bristle flat brush

MAKE MAJUN. After the majun has been scored and thoroughly cooled, use 1 of 2 techniques:

1. Gold leaf comes with tissue between the leaves. Pick up the leaf by the tissue and place it, gold side down, on the majun. Burnish the leaf on through the paper. Gold leaf is very thin (one ounce of gold makes enough to cover an acre), so it can be frustrating to handle. This method is sort of like putting on one of those fake tattoos but more stressful. In the end it looks really sophisticated. Cut and serve.

2. Gold dust is much easier to apply and it looks better, too, but it's harder to find. Simply dust a thin layer onto the majun with a brush. Cut and serve.

THE BRE-X GOLD RUSH: *Edible gold leaf is available from baking supply wholesalers and some Indian food stores (ask for Varak), or, if you're lucky, perhaps at a gourmet baking store. Gold dust is harder to find, but it's worth hunting it down because one bottle can last for years and years, depending on your lust for Bre-X bars.*

POST MAJUN BHANG: *Bhang is a cold weed tea from India that was reportedly made to honour Shiva. Here is the bastard child of that holy drink: heat the majun-soiled skillet and pour in a cup or so of milk. Stir with a wooden spoon, scraping along the sides and bottom, until the milk comes to a boil. Remove from the heat and drink.*

COUNTRY STYLE POT STORY

The morning after a party, Robin's Grandma came to visit.

"That gingerbread cake looks delicious!" she exclaimed. "May I have some?"

Pierre tried to explain the cake had pot in it, but Grandma didn't really understand and bolted a piece down before we could stop her.

Later, driving home in her car, she suffered an acute attack of paranoia. After her recovery she spent an enjoyable evening at home.

"I guess it's okay if people eat pot," conceded Grandma. "My rheumatism was all gone!"

COOKING WITH WEED$

Impressive Salmon BBQ

Invite your stoner friends over for this Pacific Northwest frolic.

5-lb. wild salmon (preferably sockeye or coho), cut into
  2 fillets

juice of one lemon

1/2 cup cannabis shake

3 tbsp. melted butter (optional)

salt and pepper to taste

GET YOUR BARBECUE READY to a medium low heat.

Squirt the lemon juice onto the fish and sprinkle it with salt and pepper. Place it skin side down onto a greased piece of foil and put it in the barbecue. Close the lid.

Barbecuing salmon generally takes about 15 minutes per inch of fillet thickness. A 5-pound salmon will split into 2 fillets that average 1 inch in thickness, therefore they will take about 15 minutes to cook.

A white milky substance will begin to form on the fillets when they are approaching doneness. When this happens, invite your stoner dinner guests to gather around the barbecue and admire the feast they are about to consume; perhaps remind them that they just might be the last generation that gets to eat wild salmon. Now, sprinkle the shake onto the coals. Bask in the smoke and try to take a toke. No one gets stoned but who cares since there's barbecued wild salmon to eat.

Some people like to brush melted butter onto the salmon after it's taken off the barbecue.

Makes 8 servings.

TALK TO THE FISHMONGER: *Instead of fooling around with all that filleting and boning and scaling at home, get the accommodating monger at the fish market to do it for you. He won't mind; it's all in a day's work.*

POULTRYGEIST 2

PIERRE, I KNOW YOU'RE UPSET ABOUT THE CHICKEN, BUT I WISH YOU'D STOP **RIPPING UP** MY COMICS WHILE I'M ASLEEP

? I **DON'T**

WELL, THERE'S ONLY **2** PEOPLE HERE, AND **1** OF THEM IS DOING IT, AND IT'S **NOT ME**...

I **DIDN'T** DO IT

—IT MUST BE THE **GHOST** OF THE **CHICKEN**

OH, COME OFF IT, PIERRE!

DON'T EXPECT ME TO **FALL** FOR THAT HIPPIE **MUMBO JUMBO**

I **KNOW** IT'S YOU WHO'S DOING IT

I AM **NOT!** AND IT'S **NOT** MUMBO JUMBO

WHEN PEOPLE DIE **VIOLENT** DEATHS SOMETIMES THEIR **GHOST COMES BACK**

THEIR SPIRIT FEELS ALL **RESTLESS** BECAUSE THEY HAVE **UNFINISHED BUSINESS** ON EARTH

BUT IT WAS A **CHICKEN**

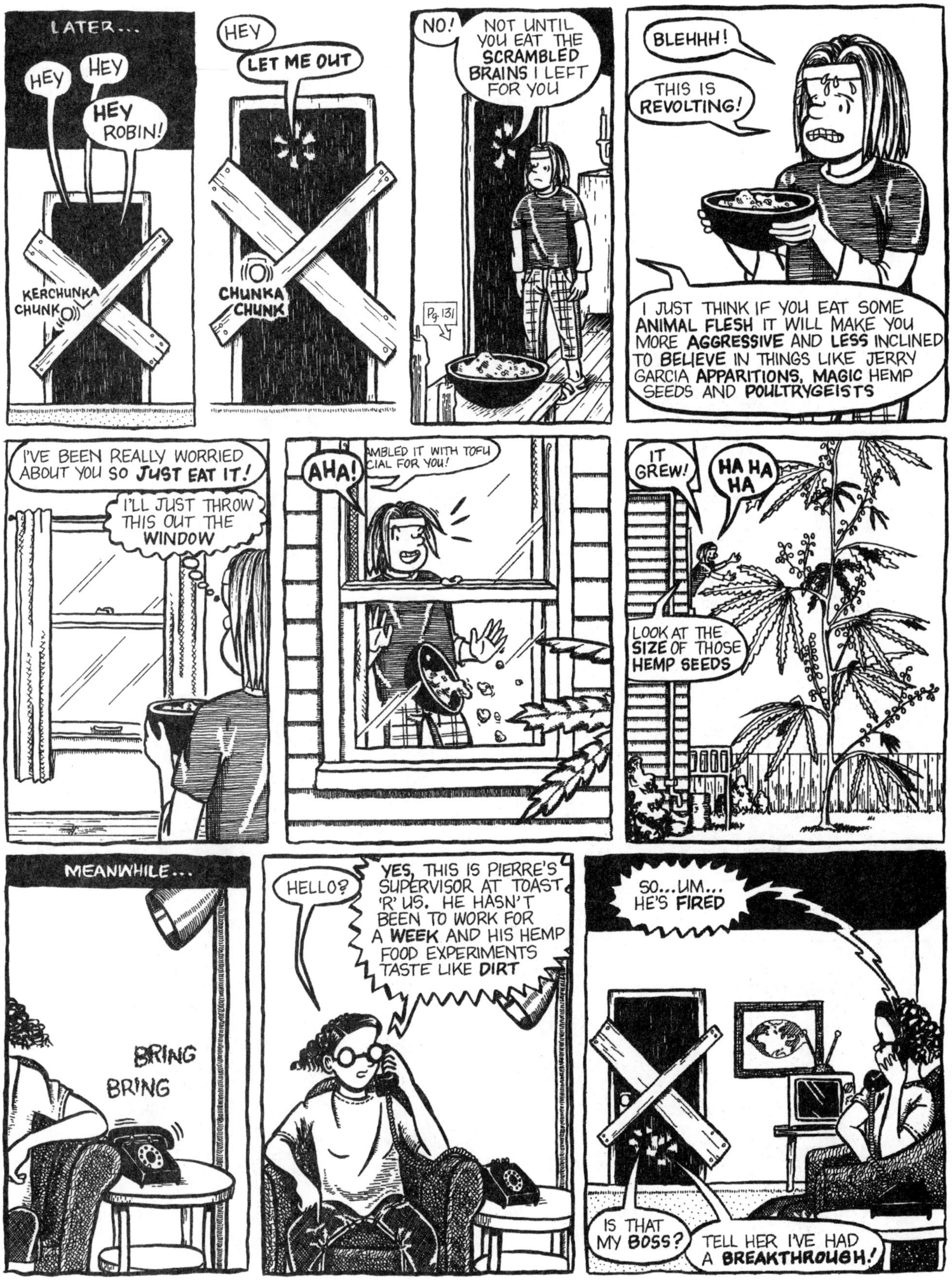
LATER...
HEY
HEY
HEY ROBIN!
KERCHUNKA CHUNK
HEY
LET ME OUT
CHUNKA CHUNK
NO!
NOT UNTIL YOU EAT THE SCRAMBLED BRAINS I LEFT FOR YOU
Pg. 131
BLEHHH!
THIS IS REVOLTING!
I JUST THINK IF YOU EAT SOME ANIMAL FLESH IT WILL MAKE YOU MORE AGGRESSIVE AND LESS INCLINED TO BELIEVE IN THINGS LIKE JERRY GARCIA APPARITIONS, MAGIC HEMP SEEDS AND POULTRYGEISTS
I'VE BEEN REALLY WORRIED ABOUT YOU SO JUST EAT IT!
I'LL JUST THROW THIS OUT THE WINDOW
AMBLED IT WITH TOFU
CIAL FOR YOU!
AHA!
IT GREW!
HA HA HA
LOOK AT THE SIZE OF THOSE HEMP SEEDS
MEANWHILE...
BRING
BRING
HELLO?
YES, THIS IS PIERRE'S SUPERVISOR AT TOAST 'R' US. HE HASN'T BEEN TO WORK FOR A WEEK AND HIS HEMP FOOD EXPERIMENTS TASTE LIKE DIRT
SO...UM... HE'S FIRED
IS THAT MY BOSS?
TELL HER I'VE HAD A BREAKTHROUGH!

INSTRUCTIONS: ① MAKE **MAJUN**, PG.122, AND WRAP EACH PIECE IN PLASTIC ② **CUT OUT** THE STONEROOKA PIERRE COMICS ALONG THE DOTTED LINES ③ **FOLD** COMICS LENGTHWISE AND **WRAP** ONE AROUND EACH PIECE OF MAJUN ④ **WRAP** AGAIN IN BRIGHTLY COLOURED FOIL ⑤ GIVE AWAY

DRAWINGS FROM ROBIN K. JOKES STOLEN FROM ASSORTED EIGHT YEAR OLDS

Stonerooka Pierre AND HIS SIDEKICK DUMPY ROBIN

NOTE TO THE LAWABIDING: IT'S **TOTALLY ILLEGAL** TO REPRODUCE THIS PAGE, SO **DON'T** PHOTOCOPY IT. YOU'LL HAVE TO **CUT** IT **OUT** OF THIS BOOK AND BE SATISFIED WITH **6** GIFT MAJUNS.(FOR MORE GIFT MAJUNS BUY MORE COPIES). HOWEVER, IT'S A MOOT POINT SINCE MAJUN IS A **TOTALLY ILLEGAL** CANDY SO YOU'D **NEVER** MAKE IT **ANYWAY**, YOU SPINELESS WUSS.

Bad Trade

These pages contain the most obnoxious recipes to come out of the *Scrambled Brains* Laboratory. "What is the use of that?" cries the observant reader. No use, except that we at *Scrambled Brains* wish to cross the boundaries of bad taste to embrace the repugnant.

Why? Because it's bad trade, baby.

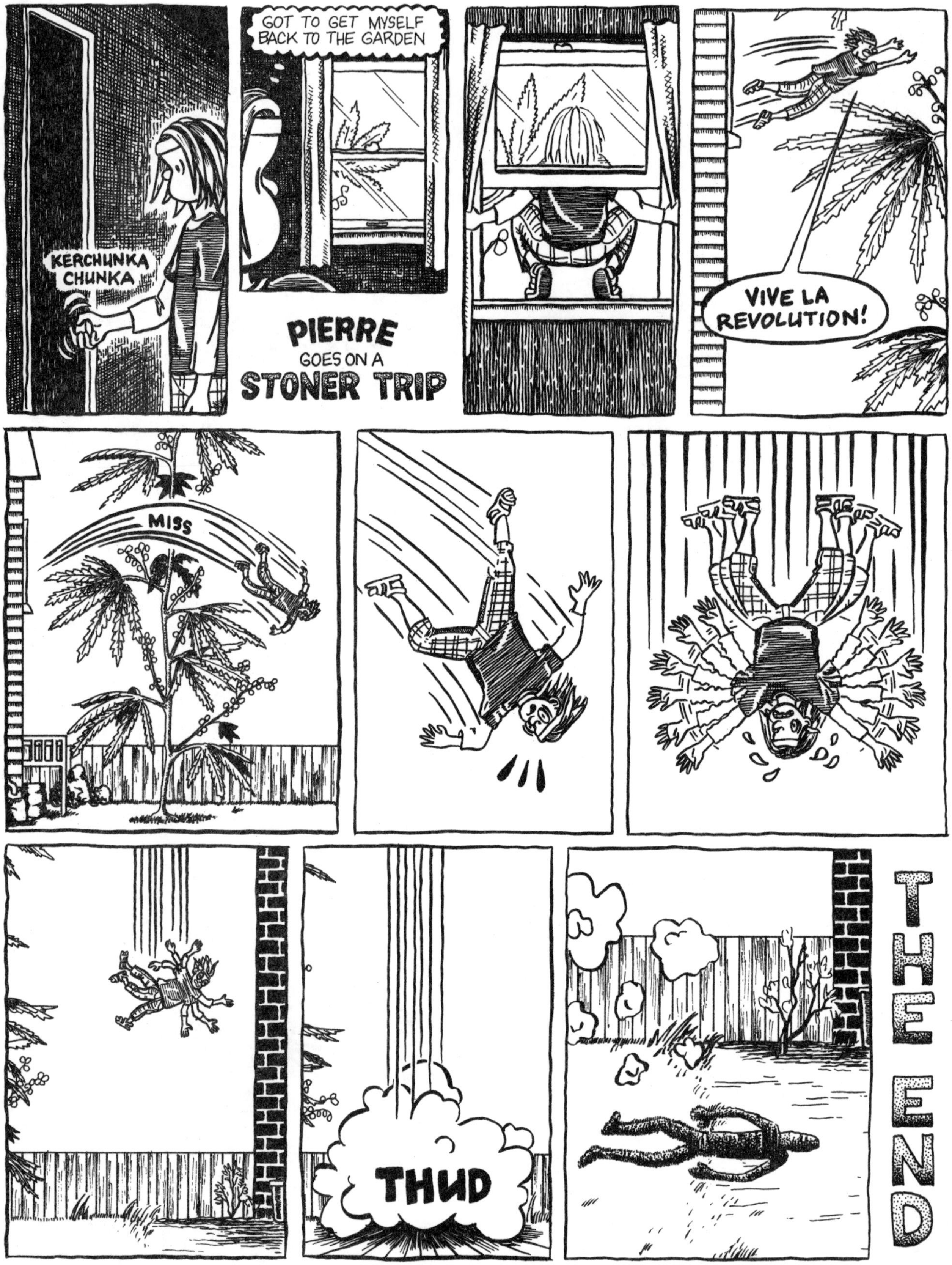
KERCHUNKA CHUNKA
GOT TO GET MYSELF BACK TO THE GARDEN
PIERRE GOES ON A STONER TRIP
VIVE LA REVOLUTION!
MISS
THUD
THE END

Scrambled Brains

Carnage and prepackaged food meet with tofu in contemporary confusion cuisine.

1 lb. fresh veal brains

6 cups water

pinch of thyme

2 bay leaves

1 lb. soft tofu, cut into 4 pieces

2/3 envelope Tofu Scrambler instant seasoning powder

3 tbsp. butter

salt and pepper to taste

PLACE THE BRAINS in a large pot and cover them with the water. Add the thyme, bay leaves, and some salt and bring it to a boil. Let simmer for 25 minutes.

Drain the brains and discard the poaching water. Then chill the brains in an ice water bath for 3 minutes. Cut it into 1/4-inch cubes.

In a large cast-iron skillet or non-stick frying pan over medium high heat, melt the butter until it starts to turn brown. Add the tofu cubes and stir until it begins to resemble anaemic scrambled eggs. Gradually stir in the instant seasoning powder. When everything in the pan is steaming hot, add the brain cubes and cook for another 3 minutes, stirring constantly.

Season to taste and serve immediately.

Supposedly makes 6 servings, but when we made it only 2 people had 1 bite each and no one else would touch it, including us.

COLLECTING A BRAIN

Depending on your location fresh brains might be a difficult thing to buy, but one thing that's certain is there's a slaughterhouse near you. So we suggest you ask your local meat pusher to call up the boys there and get them to crack a few skulls.

BRAINS DON'T LAST

Brains are very rich and not particularly nutritious. They are also extremely perishable, so be sure to consume them fresh. More than likely when you receive a brain it is full of blood and gore, so to drain out the blood leave it under cold running water for an hour or, for the more eco-conscious of you, soak it in an ice water bath with a few tablespoons of salt and vinegar in it. After this process you should remove the fatty tissue around the brain before poaching.

SCRAMBLED BRAINS

Robin's Grandpa used to amuse himself by trying to gross her out. One of the most nauseating things he would do was cook scrambled brains. First he would go to the fridge and get the dreaded paper "brain bag," all the while describing the different types of animal brains you can eat. He would go into minute detail about various butchering methods, and uses for the less appetizing bits of the animal carcass, especially brains. Beef brains, pork brains, lamb brains. His preference was for the the sweet and tender brain of the baby cow. He would chop the brains with a meat cleaver, laughing maniacally the whole time. When they were ready he would try to make Robin eat them. She never would, so he'd eat them with gusto in front of her. Then he'd tell her stories about the Depression and say, "You young kids don't know nothin'."

Well, Grandpa's dead now, and with him died his extensive knowledge of traditional brain recipes and related trivia. To commemorate Grandpa, Robin eats hot dogs on the 7th day.

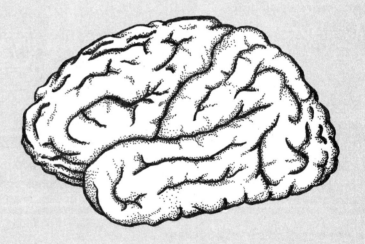

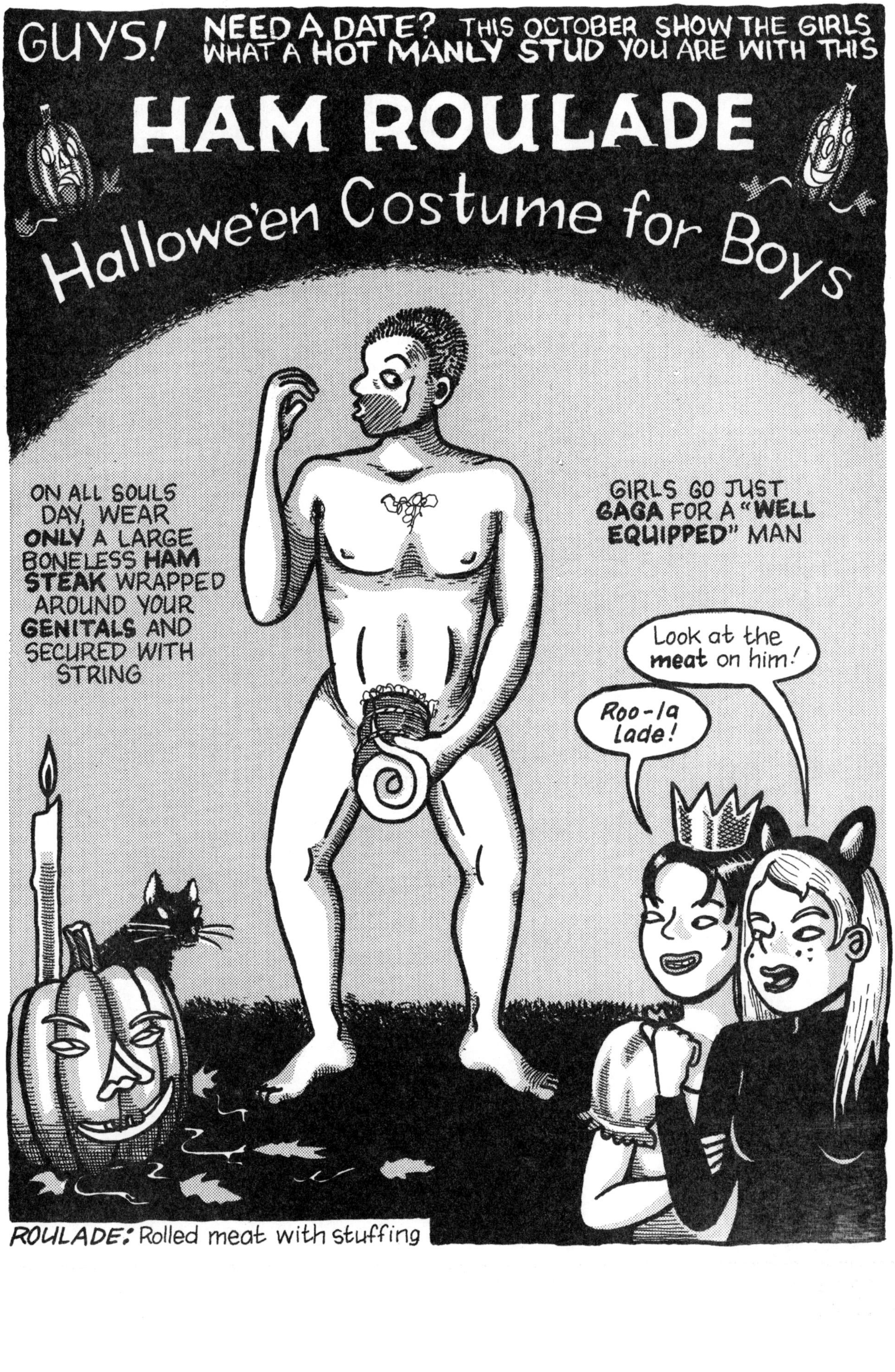
GUYS! NEED A DATE? THIS OCTOBER SHOW THE GIRLS WHAT A HOT MANLY STUD YOU ARE WITH THIS
HAM ROULADE
Hallowe'en Costume for Boys
ON ALL SOULS DAY, WEAR ONLY A LARGE BONELESS HAM STEAK WRAPPED AROUND YOUR GENITALS AND SECURED WITH STRING
GIRLS GO JUST GAGA FOR A "WELL EQUIPPED" MAN
Look at the meat on him!
Roo-la lade!

ROULADE: Rolled meat with stuffing

HOW TO BE A SUPERSTAR

Once Pierre and Robin lived with Gretchen, an exotic German chick who looked really alternative but was conservative at heart. She desired to lead an upper-middle-class lifestyle, and her future plans included marriage to a dentist, although there were none about at present.

In the meantime she decided to have a party. With her upper-crust sensibilities she hankered for some fancy *hors d'oeuvres* but she couldn't actually afford to make any, so she asked the guests to bring their own. "Bring *hors d'oeuvres* and be a star!" read the invitation.

Kathy O never really grooved on Gretchen or her friends—she thought they were a bunch of pretentious phonies. Still, she was pals with Pierre and Robin, so she came to the party anyway and even brought some paté moulded into a star. The presentation of the paté was so lovely, Gretchen placed it in the middle of the buffet table for all of her friends to enjoy.

Being the affluent lot that they were they quickly scarfed down the attractive paté. Kathy herself said she was full of it and went into the living room to put Iggy Pop on the stereo.

"This song sure brings back memories," said Robin to Kathy. "♪♪I'm living on DOG FOOOOOD♪♪ . ."

"I think in the future it will bring back even more memories," said Kathy, then told Robin her paté was made of gourmet vegetarian dog food.

"Why, that's shocking!" Robin laughed.

Somehow someone found out about the dog food paté, and the next day Gretchen's high falutin' friends were phoning to ask, "Was that really dog food we ate?"

They were disgusted. Pierre and Robin knew it was awful but they still laugh about it to this day.

BAD TRADE

Star Shaped Paté

This is a recipe for bourgeois potluck parties.

1 can gourmet vegetarian dog food

1 tbsp. capers

a few sprigs of parsley

EMPTY THE DOG FOOD into a bowl, then mash it up with a fork to break it down a bit and get the texture consistent. Then, on your nicest plate, shape the dog food into a star. Garnish it with capers and parsley sprigs.

Chill and serve with crackers or crustini.

Serves them right.

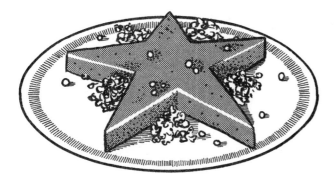

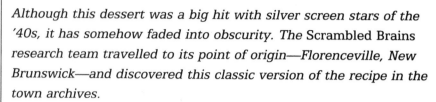
THE GALLOPING GOURMAND

Since the cake is frozen there's no need to chill the Baby Duck before serving, so you can even make this in the parking lot of the liquor store.

Although this dessert was a big hit with silver screen stars of the '40s, it has somehow faded into obscurity. The Scrambled Brains research team travelled to its point of origin—Florenceville, New Brunswick—and discovered this classic version of the recipe in the town archives.

1 McCain's frozen cake

1 bottle of Baby Duck sparkling rosé wine

6 large plastic cups

Divide the frozen cake into 6 pieces and place each piece into a plastic cup. Top up the cup with some Baby Duck right before serving.

Serves no one.

SPACE CADETS iN THE REAL END

BY ROBIN I WAS JUST KIDDING ABOUT THAT OTHER ONE BEING THE END KONSTABARIS

YOU DIDN'T EAT YOUR DIN-DINS, SO YOU DON'T GET ANY BREAKFAST

WHAT ARE YOU DOING, ROBIN?

AHH! HOW DID YOU GET OUT OF YOUR ROOM?

I JUMPED OUT THE WINDOW

SEE! THAT'S WHAT HAPPENS WHEN YOU'RE A HIPPIE AND YOU SMOKE TOO MUCH POT

YOU BELIEVE YOU CAN FLY!

I WASN'T TRYING TO FLY

I WANTED TO GET TO THE MAGIC HEMP PLANT

SEE! THAT'S WHAT HAPPENS WHEN YOU'RE A HIPPIE AND YOU SMOKE TOO MUCH POT

YOU HALLUCINATE MAGIC HEMP PLANTS!

ROBIN, LEAVE ME ALONE. I JUST HAD A NEAR DEATH EXPERIENCE AND I'M NOT A HIPPIE ANYMORE

NEAR DEATH! IT'S ONLY 1 STORY

IT WAS REALLY SCARY

I CAN'T BELIEVE I ALMOST KILLED MYSELF OVER SOME STUPID IDEALS I DON'T EVEN BELIEVE IN

LIKE WHAT?

LIKE PEACE, LOVE, AND SPIRITUALITY

HE'S ALL BITTER, POOR THING

I'VE COME TO REALIZE MY WHOLE HIPPIE PHASE WAS JUST A DESPERATE GRAB AT AN INSTANT IDENTITY

I JUST FEEL I HAVE NO CONTROL OR DIRECTION IN MY LIFE

FOR INSTANCE, I WOULD NEVER HAVE GUESSED I WOULD END UP AS A HEMP FOOD RESEARCHER, MUCH LESS STYLE MY LIFE AROUND IT

OH, THAT REMINDS ME. YOUR BOSS FROM TOAST 'R' US PHONED

YOU'RE FIRED!

OH, GREAT! JUST WHEN I HAD A BREAKTHROUGH

WELL, WHAT DO YOU EXPECT FROM A COMPANY WITH A GRAMMATICAL ERROR IN THEIR NAME?

MAYBE I CAN FREE-LANCE FOR THEM. I STILL HAVE THESE SEEDS

GOOD LORD!

THERE'S A HU-MUNGOUS HEMP PLANT IN THE BACK YARD

THAT'S IT! THAT'S THE MAGIC HEMP PLANT

I'M HALLUCINATING

NOW I'M HALLU-CINATING THAT THERE ARE 6 POLICE OFFICERS IN OUR YARD

AHHH IT'S A BUST

THEY'RE CHOPPING DOWN THE HEMP PLANT

QUICK! HELP ME FLUSH THIS POT DOWN THE TOILET

NOW THEY'RE CUTTING IT UP INTO LITTLE ITTY BITS

AHH! FLUSH, D@#! YOU

THEY'RE ROLLING SOME INTO A BIG JOINT

HOW STUPID!

IT'S AN INDUSTRIAL PLANT

IT HARDLY HAS ANY THC IN IT.

WHY WOULD I HALLUCINATE THAT, I WONDER?

GET OUT OF THE WAY!

NOW THEY'RE COUGHING

S#!T S#!T S#!T

NOW THEY'RE LEAVING

CALM DOWN, PIERRE

REALLY? OH NO!

I FLUSHED THE POT DOWN THE TOILET!

OH WELL EASY COME, EASY GO

LORDY! IF I HAD DREAMS I'D BE CRUSHED NOW

I'M GLAD YOU'RE NOT A HIPPIE ANYMORE, PIERRE

ME TOO. I FELT LIKE A POSEUR AND I COULD NEVER QUITE GET THE LINGO DOWN

PECK

OW!

BUT ON THE OTHER HAND IT FELT GOOD TO HAVE A PURPOSE IN LIFE, NO MATTER HOW RIDICULOUS

YEAH, I HAD FUN WHILE I WAS A PRINCESS

SIGH

I JUST DON'T KNOW HOW TO DEAL WITH THESE DEEPLY INGRAINED FEELINGS OF INSIGNIFICANCE AND INADEQUACY

I KNOW

PERSONALLY, I DEAL WITH THEM BY GETTING TOTALLY INVOLVED AND OBSESSED WITH CHILDISH, DEAD END PURSUITS SUCH AS DRAWING COMICS

A PHANTOM EGG ←

DOES THAT HELP?

NO. IN FACT, IF ANYTHING IT ONLY SERVES TO ACCENTUATE MY FEELINGS OF ALIENATION FROM THE REST OF SOCIETY

WHY DO IT, THEN?

TO DISTRACT MYSELF FROM MY FRUSTRATION WITH THE ABSURDITY OF THE HUMAN CONDITION

DOES THAT WORK?

NOT REALLY. BUT IT'S STILL SORT OF FUN. I GET TO BE THE ALL MASTER OF REALITY

YEAH, I GUESS I SHOULD DO SOMETHING, BUT I CAN'T THINK OF WHAT...

WE'RE BOTH JOBLESS. LET'S HITCHHIKE TO ALASKA

ALASKA OR BUST

NAH

REMEMBER THAT BOOK IDEA I HAD? WE COULD DO THAT.

NAH

HOW ABOUT REDECORATING THE BATHROOM?

NAH

HEY! THERE'S A BIG MARY JANE BUD ON THE BATHROOM FLOOR!

WANNA SMOKE A JOINT?

OKAY

ACTUALLY IT NEVER ENDS

Glossary

Bâtons: A French cooking term meaning vegetables cut into small stick shapes.

Blanch: To plunge vegetables or fruit into boiling water momentarily, then immediately into a bath of cold water to seal in nutrients and colour.

Bon D'Jeux: Acadian slang for "Good God."

Brown roux: A roux that is cooked until the mixture turns brown.

Bud: The flower of the female marijuana plant, it contains the greatest concentration of THC.

Cannabis sativa: A weed that grows wild in many parts of the world, also known as marijuana.

Caramel: A clear liquid produced when sugar is melted.

Caramelize: The process of heating sugar or rendering the sugar contained in certain foods, such as onions.

Celeriac: Also know as celery root, it tastes like a cross between a parsnip and a celery.

Chiffonade: To cut into paper-thin strips with a sharp knife or scissors.

Chorizo: A spicy Spanish sausage made with pork, garlic, and hot chilies.

Condiment: A sauce, relish, or spice to accompany and season food.

Coulis: A thick purée or sauce.

Crudités: Raw vegetables, normally served as an appetizer.

Deglaze: To pour a small amount of liquid into a hot pan to reclaim the juicy crusties on the bottom. A method often used for soups and sauces.

Dice: To chop into small or tiny cubes.

Doob: A marijuana cigarette.

Egg Wash: A beaten egg brushed onto pastry or bread before baking to give it a shine.

Fatty: A large marijuana cigarette.

4-20: Hippie code for "Light the marijuana cigarette."

Ga+cân'sa: A Vietnamese term for marijuana.

Garam masala: An Indian blend of up to 10 different spices. Usually used at the end of cooking a recipe to even out the flavours and add a warm sensation to the dish.

High: Stoned out of your mind on tetrahydrocannabinol.

Hootcher: A marijuana cigarette.

Infusion: The extraction of an aroma or flavour from an ingredient by steeping it in a liquid; e.g., tea and flavoured vinegars.

Jardinière: A variety of steamed vegetables served to garnish a main dish on a platter.

Jerusalem artichokes: A root vegetable native to North America. They are actually sunflower tubers, and kind of taste like artichokes.

Joint: A marijuana cigarette.

Julienne: A style of vegetable chopping, named after chef Jean Julienne, who cut his vegetables into thin sticks.

Kecap Manis: A thick Indonesian soy sauce that is sweetened with palm sugar.

Kit: An outfit of clothing.

Lime leaves: The leaves of the lime tree, which can be used to bring a distinctive citrus aroma to soups and sauces.

Lovage: Also known as bastard celery, this is an old-fashioned herb that resembles a celery plant growing out of control. Its seed is commonly sold as celery seed.

Mary Jane: Dried *cannabis sativa* bud.

Mince: To render into a paste by chopping or crushing.

Miso: A fermented soy bean paste originating from Japan, where it is used extensively in soups, dressings, and sauces.

Ostentatious: Showy.

Palm sugar: Unrefined sugar made from the sap of palm trees that is sold in a block and used as sugar.

Poach: To cook at a low temperature in a small amount of liquid.

Reduce: To reduce the amount of liquid by evaporation.

Roux: A thickening agent consisting of cooked flour and butter.

Sauté: Derived from the French verb "to have jumped": to fry lightly and quickly while stirring or shaking the pan with regularity.

Schmooglyboogle: A small atomic explosive device which detonates instantly upon human contact.

Score: To make a superficial cut on the surface, but not through.

Seed: To remove the seeds from fruits or vegetables.

Semolina: Coarsely-ground durum wheat, used mostly in the making of pasta. Also used for other grains ground to the same consistency; e.g., corn semolina.

Shake: The leaves (usually the bottom leaves) of the marijuana plant, minus the bud.

Speculaas: A Dutch spice blend consisting of equal parts of cinnamon, cardomon, ginger, cloves, and white pepper. Mainly used in Dutch Christmas baking.

Sulk: To sit unsociably in a corner emitting an aura of dissatisfaction.

THC: Tetrahydrocannabinol—it gets you high.

Toke: A puff from a marijuana cigarette.

Tomato concassé: A skinned tomato with the seeds and juice removed, then cut into small cubes.

Wake and bake: To smoke a marijuana cigarette immediately upon waking.

Weed: Dried *cannabis sativa* buds.

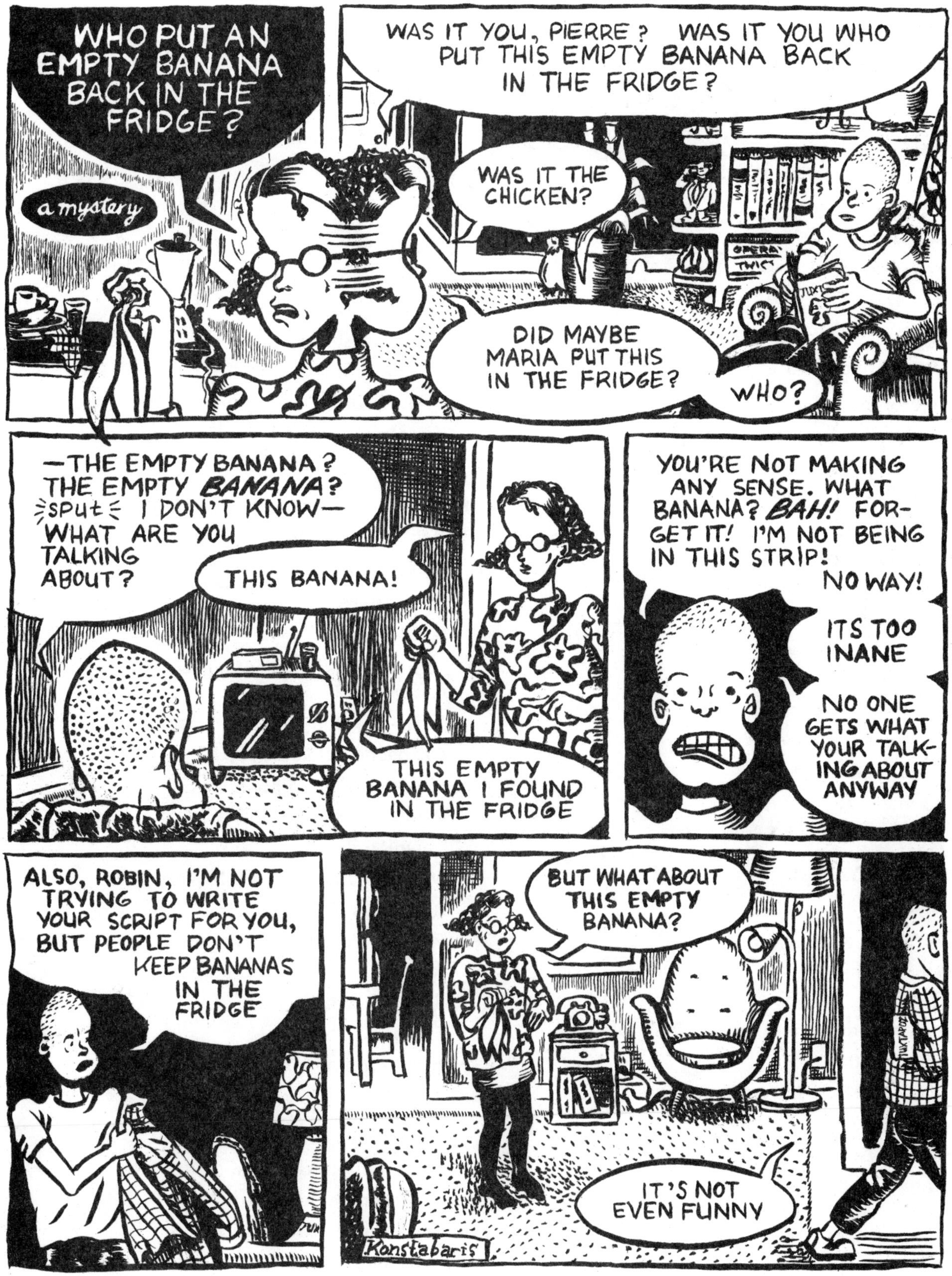

WHO PUT AN EMPTY BANANA BACK IN THE FRIDGE?
a mystery
WAS IT YOU, PIERRE? WAS IT YOU WHO PUT THIS EMPTY BANANA BACK IN THE FRIDGE?
WAS IT THE CHICKEN?
DID MAYBE MARIA PUT THIS IN THE FRIDGE?
WHO?
—THE EMPTY BANANA? THE EMPTY BANANA? sput I DON'T KNOW— WHAT ARE YOU TALKING ABOUT?
THIS BANANA!
THIS EMPTY BANANA I FOUND IN THE FRIDGE
YOU'RE NOT MAKING ANY SENSE. WHAT BANANA? BAH! FORGET IT! I'M NOT BEING IN THIS STRIP! NO WAY!
ITS TOO INANE
NO ONE GETS WHAT YOUR TALKING ABOUT ANYWAY
ALSO, ROBIN, I'M NOT TRYING TO WRITE YOUR SCRIPT FOR YOU, BUT PEOPLE DON'T KEEP BANANAS IN THE FRIDGE
BUT WHAT ABOUT THIS EMPTY BANANA?
IT'S NOT EVEN FUNNY
Konstabaris

Index

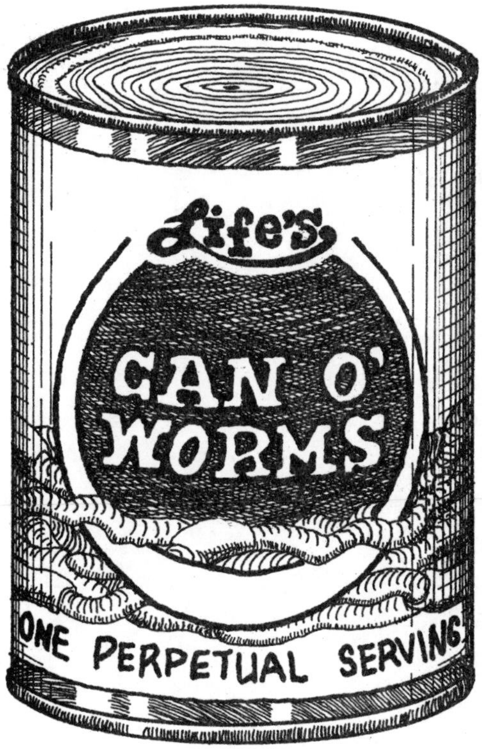

Life's
CAN O' WORMS
ONE PERPETUAL SERVING

COMICS

* Party tips

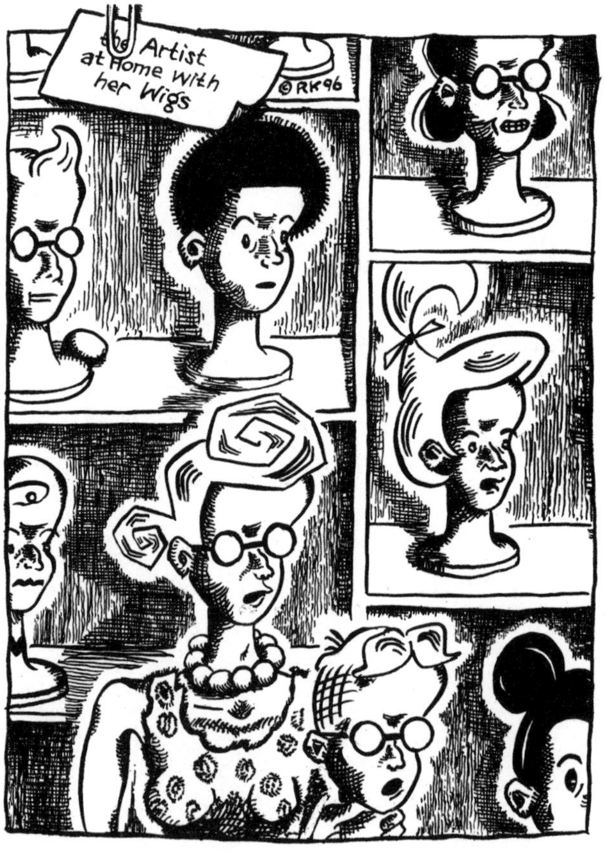

the Artist at Home with her Wigs
©RK96